OPPOSING VIEWPOINTS® SERIES

Tobacco and Smoking

Other Books of Related Interest

Opposing Viewpoints Series

Addiction

Birth Defects

Privacy

Scientific Research

At Issue Series

The Affordable Care Act

Extending the Human Lifespan

Should the Government Regulate What People Eat?

Teen Smoking

Current Controversies Series

Drug Legalization

Medical Ethics

Pesticides

Prescription Drugs

"Congress shall make no law ... abridging the freedom of speech, or of the press."

First Amendment to the US Constitution

The basic foundation of our democracy is the First Amendment guarantee of freedom of expression. The Opposing Viewpoints series is dedicated to the concept of this basic freedom and the idea that it is more important to practice it than to enshrine it.

OPPOSING VIEWPOINTS® SERIES

Tobacco and Smoking

Roman Espejo, Book Editor

GREENHAVEN PRESS
A part of Gale, Cengage Learning

GALE
CENGAGE Learning·

Farmington Hills, Mich • San Francisco • New York • Waterville, Maine
Meriden, Conn • Mason, Ohio • Chicago

GALE
CENGAGE Learning·

Patricia Coryell, *Vice President & Publisher, New Products & GVRL*
Douglas Dentino, *Manager, New Products*
Judy Galens, *Acquisitions Editor*

© 2015 Greenhaven Press, a part of Gale, Cengage Learning.

WCN: 01-100-101

Gale and Greenhaven Press are registered trademarks used herein under license.

For more information, contact:
Greenhaven Press
27500 Drake Rd.
Farmington Hills, MI 48331-3535
Or you can visit our Internet site at gale.cengage.com

Articles in Greenhaven Press anthologies are often edited for length to meet page requirements. In addition, original titles of these works are changed to clearly present the main thesis and to explicitly indicate the author's opinion. Every effort is made to ensure that Greenhaven Press accurately reflects the original intent of the authors. Every effort has been made to trace the owners of copyrighted material.

Cover Image copyright © Nordling/Shutterstock.com.

LIBRARY OF CONGRESS CATALOGING-IN-PUBLICATION DATA

Tobacco and smoking / Roman Espejo, book editor.
   pages cm. -- (Opposing viewpoints)
   Includes bibliographical references and index.
   ISBN 978-0-7377-7294-4 (hardcover) -- ISBN 978-0-7377-7295-1 (pbk.)
   1. Smoking--United States--Juvenile literature. 2. Smoking--Health aspects--United States--Juvenile literature. 3. Tobacco use--United States--Juvenile literature. 4. Teenagers--Tobacco use--United States--Juvenile literature. I. Espejo, Roman, 1977-
   HV5760.T623 2015
   362.29'6--dc23
                               2014026089

Printed in the United States of America
1 2 3 4 5 6 7 19 18 17 16 15

Contents

3/15   32.10
Gale/Cengage Learning

Chapter 3: How Should Smoking Alternatives Be Regulated?

Chapter 4: How Do Media Impact the Choice to Smoke or Not Smoke?

Why Consider Opposing Viewpoints?

> *"The only way in which a human being can make some approach to knowing the whole of a subject is by hearing what can be said about it by persons of every variety of opinion and studying all modes in which it can be looked at by every character of mind. No wise man ever acquired his wisdom in any mode but this."*
>
> *John Stuart Mill*

In our media-intensive culture it is not difficult to find differing opinions. Thousands of newspapers and magazines and dozens of radio and television talk shows resound with differing points of view. The difficulty lies in deciding which opinion to agree with and which "experts" seem the most credible. The more inundated we become with differing opinions and claims, the more essential it is to hone critical reading and thinking skills to evaluate these ideas. Opposing Viewpoints books address this problem directly by presenting stimulating debates that can be used to enhance and teach these skills. The varied opinions contained in each book examine many different aspects of a single issue. While examining these conveniently edited opposing views, readers can develop critical thinking skills such as the ability to compare and contrast authors' credibility, facts, argumentation styles, use of persuasive techniques, and other stylistic tools. In short, the Opposing Viewpoints Series is an ideal way to attain the higher-level thinking and reading skills so essential in a culture of diverse and contradictory opinions.

In addition to providing a tool for critical thinking, Opposing Viewpoints books challenge readers to question their own strongly held opinions and assumptions. Most people form their opinions on the basis of upbringing, peer pressure, and personal, cultural, or professional bias. By reading carefully balanced opposing views, readers must directly confront new ideas as well as the opinions of those with whom they disagree. This is not to argue simplistically that everyone who reads opposing views will—or should—change his or her opinion. Instead, the series enhances readers' understanding of their own views by encouraging confrontation with opposing ideas. Careful examination of others' views can lead to the readers' understanding of the logical inconsistencies in their own opinions, perspective on why they hold an opinion, and the consideration of the possibility that their opinion requires further evaluation.

Evaluating Other Opinions

To ensure that this type of examination occurs, Opposing Viewpoints books present all types of opinions. Prominent spokespeople on different sides of each issue as well as well-known professionals from many disciplines challenge the reader. An additional goal of the series is to provide a forum for other, less known, or even unpopular viewpoints. The opinion of an ordinary person who has had to make the decision to cut off life support from a terminally ill relative, for example, may be just as valuable and provide just as much insight as a medical ethicist's professional opinion. The editors have two additional purposes in including these less known views. One, the editors encourage readers to respect others' opinions—even when not enhanced by professional credibility. It is only by reading or listening to and objectively evaluating others' ideas that one can determine whether they are worthy of consideration. Two, the inclusion of such viewpoints encourages the important critical thinking skill of objectively evaluating an author's credentials and bias. This evaluation will illuminate an author's reasons for taking a particular stance on an issue and will aid in readers' evaluation of the author's ideas.

It is our hope that these books will give readers a deeper understanding of the issues debated and an appreciation of the complexity of even seemingly simple issues when good and honest people disagree. This awareness is particularly important in a democratic society such as ours in which people enter into public debate to determine the common good. Those with whom one disagrees should not be regarded as enemies but rather as people whose views deserve careful examination and may shed light on one's own.

Thomas Jefferson once said that "difference of opinion leads to inquiry, and inquiry to truth." Jefferson, a broadly educated man, argued that "if a nation expects to be ignorant and free . . . it expects what never was and never will be." As individuals and as a nation, it is imperative that we consider the opinions of others and examine them with skill and discernment. The Opposing Viewpoints series is intended to help readers achieve this goal.

David L. Bender and Bruno Leone,
Founders

Introduction

"Cigar smoke, like cigarette smoke, contains toxic and cancer-causing chemicals that are harmful to both smokers and nonsmokers."

—National Cancer Institute

"It has been demonstrated that the sales curve of cigars (unlike that of cigarettes) has never approached a strong statistical association with the incidence of . . . various health-related problems."

—James Weiss,
"Opinion: Cigar Smoking
and Coronary Health,"
Cigar Aficionado, Winter 1994

In 2011, 13.7 billion cigars were sold in the United States— 12.9 billion large cigars and cigarillos and 0.8 billion small cigars. Additionally, premium cigars make up 60 percent of total domestic sales. Imperial Tobacco, a global company based in the United Kingdom, asserts that this particular segment of the market is on the rise. "After the significant rebound experienced by this industry in 2010 and 2011, when sales grew by 10% after the economic crisis, luxury fundamentals are expecting to remain strong in the next coming years," says Fernando Domínguez, premium cigar director for Imperial Tobacco.

While its exact origins remain unknown, the cigar can be traced back more than a millennium. A Mayan artifact from the tenth century—a ceramic pot with an image of a figure smoking bound leaves of tobacco—was found in Guatemala. In fact, the Spanish term *cigarro* comes from *sikar*, the Mayan word for smoking. Furthermore, when explorer Christopher Columbus sailed to the Americas in 1492, he encountered indigenous people puffing on tobacco in corn husks or palm leaves; thought to have medicinal properties, tobacco was brought back to Europe by sailors. "Spain developed quite the appetite for cigars, one that exceeded its ability to produce them, leading to Spanish investment in its then-colony of Cuba, where cigar production began in earnest," explains David Savona in a September 2012 article in *Cigar Aficionado*.

As the use of tobacco spread throughout Europe and beyond, in 1717, Philip V of Spain ordered a Spanish monopoly of the Cuban cigar industry that lasted for a century. By the mid-1800s, Americans had consumed three hundred million cigars, with numerous Cuban tobacco producers settling in Florida. However, since the early 1960s, cigars from Cuba—prized by enthusiasts—have been blocked from importation in the United States due to its embargo against the Caribbean nation, changing the industry and the cigar itself. "When U.S. President John F. Kennedy signed an embargo prohibiting nearly all trade between Cuba and the United States in 1962, it forced cigar makers to reinvent their blends. Cuban leaf, the lifeblood of the cigar industry, was now off-limits to American smokers," explains Savona. Despite the sanctions, Cuban cigar making has grown to a $500 million business.

As a tobacco product, cigars are associated with serious and lethal health hazards. "Cigars contain the same addictive, toxic, and carcinogenic compounds found in cigarettes," asserts the American Lung Association. "In fact, a single large cigar can contain as much tobacco as an entire pack of cigarettes." The association warns that cigar smokers are at high risk of developing various cancers, from the lungs to the oral cavity. Moreover, although cigar smoke is not inhaled and held in the mouth, it is argued that cigars are not a safer alternative for cigarette smokers. "Because of its chemical makeup, cigars can send nicotine to the brain even if the smoke isn't inhaled," maintains Lynn T. Kozlowski, former dean of the School of Public Health and Health Professions at the University at Buffalo, the State University of New York, in a July 18, 2013, article for the *Huffington Post*. Citing a study published in *Preventive Medicine*, he observes that when smoking cigars, former cigarette smokers use them like cigarettes, sticking to the same habits. "Cigarette smokers who switched to cigars often kept on inhaling smoke, and they also often smoked more cigars per day than cigar smokers who never smoked cigarettes. Cigarette smokers who switch to daily cigar smoking (or pipe smoking) and who inhale, should not expect to cut their health risks," Kozlowski points out.

Nonetheless, other commentators propose that cigars, while unhealthy, are still safer than cigarettes. According to Geoffrey Cowley, a national writer covering health policy for MSNBC.com, the dangers are not equal. "Cigarette smokers are roughly 20 times more likely than nonsmokers to develop lung cancer, and four times more likely to suffer from coronary artery disease," he claims. "Even the most dedicated cigar smokers experience only a threefold increase in lung-cancer risk (mainly from living around their own fumes) and a doubling of stroke and heart-attack risk." Referring to a study of twenty-two thousand participants published in the *British Medical Journal*, Cowley adds that those who switched to cigars from cigarettes "enjoyed a 50 percent reduction in risk of death from lung cancer, heart disease and chronic obstructive lung disease—mainly because they smoked less after they switched." How much cigar smokers actually light up—compared to cigarette smokers—is also debated. "The great majority of cigar smokers smoke fewer than one cigar per day and don't inhale," insists physician Marc J. Schneiderman in the 1998 report "A Response to the NCI Report—Cigars: Health Effects and Trends." Schneiderman continues, "The 'habitual' cigar smoker is rarely even a daily smoker."

Cigars are just one of the many types of tobacco products manufactured today. Newer and more novel items—electronic cigarettes, hookahs, snus—have gained recent attention as smokers search for reportedly safer, less expensive, or easier ways to get their nicotine fixes. *Opposing Viewpoints: Tobacco and Smoking* examines the risks of tobacco products, the purported benefits of the alternatives to smoking, and the policies intended to reduce the habit and regulate the industry in chapters titled "Is Tobacco Use a Serious Problem?," "How Can Tobacco Use Be Reduced?," "How Should Smoking Alternatives Be Regulated?," and "How Do Media Impact the Choice to Smoke or Not Smoke?" The diverse opinions and conflicting analyses presented in this volume attest to tobacco as one of the most controversial legal substances.

OPPOSING
VIEWPOINTS®
SERIES

CHAPTER 1

Is Tobacco Use a Serious Problem?

Chapter Preface

Smoking cigarettes causes 90 percent of all lung cancers, claims the Centers for Disease Control and Prevention (CDC). "People who smoke are fifteen to thirty times more likely to get lung cancer or die from lung cancer than people who do not smoke. Even smoking a few cigarettes a day or smoking occasionally increases the risk of lung cancer," the CDC maintains. Individuals who quit smoking still have a higher chance of developing lung cancer than those who have never smoked. "The more years a person smokes and the more cigarettes smoked each day, the more risk goes up," the CDC states.

In 2010—the latest statistics cited by the CDC—201,144 Americans were diagnosed with lung cancer; 107,164 were men and 93,980 were women. That same year, 158,248 Americans died from the disease; 87,698 were men and 70,550 were women. "More people in the United States die from lung cancer than any other type of cancer. This is true for both men and women," declares the CDC.

Nonetheless, it is proposed that smoking may not be the only factor contributing to lung cancer. Leslie Pray, a science writer with a doctoral degree in population genetics, states that a person's genes can also play a role. She explains, "In recent years, three independent groups of international scientists have identified a region on chromosome 15 that, if mutated, dramatically increases a smoker's risk of developing lung cancer by another 30% to 80% (giving smokers who carry this mutation an overall lung cancer risk of about 20% to 23%), depending on whether an individual has one or two copies of what the researchers are calling the 15q24 susceptibility locus." Pray reiterates, however, that tobacco places people at risk of the disease no matter what. "Remember, even smokers without the locus have a tenfold greater risk of developing lung cancer than nonsmokers do. In other words, all smokers are at risk of lung cancer, but some smokers are a greater risk than others," she states. In the following chapter, the authors examine tobacco and smoking as a public health issue.

"Smoking is the chief preventable cause of premature death in this country."

Tobacco Use Is a Serious Problem

US Department of Health and Human Services

The US Department of Health and Human Services (HHS) is the federal government's principal agency for protecting the health of Americans and providing essential human services. In the following viewpoint, HHS maintains that tobacco use is epidemic among youths and young adults. Despite decades of research identifying smoking with immediate and long-term health consequences, the department states, about one in four high school seniors smokes, and one million Americans become new smokers each year. In fact, HHS continues, smoking is the nation's leading cause of preventable, premature death, and many young smokers already exhibit the early stages of smoking-related diseases found in adults. While some rates of tobacco use have decreased in the late 1990s to the mid-2000s, the department recommends reinvigorating efforts to combat the use of tobacco for future generations.

"Preventing Tobacco Use Among Youth and Young Adults: A Report of the Surgeon General: Executive Summary," US Department of Health and Human Services, 2012, pp. 1–7.

As you read, consider the following questions:

1. What figures does HHS provide for high school smokers who are unable to break from nicotine addiction?

2. Research documents what strong causal associations with cigarette smoking and nicotine addiction in young people, as stated by HHS?

3. How does HHS describe the prevalence of tobacco use among young people in recent years?

Tobacco use is a pediatric epidemic, around the world as well as in the United States. Although progress has been made since the first surgeon general's report in 1964, too many of our youth still use tobacco. Among U.S. high school seniors, one out of four is a regular cigarette smoker. Because few high school smokers are able to break free from the powerful addicting effects of nicotine, about 80% will smoke into adulthood. Among those who persist in smoking, one-half will die about 13 years earlier than his or her nonsmoking peers.

In addition to cigarette smoking, use of other forms of tobacco by youth and young adults is epidemic. Nearly one in five white adolescent males (12–17 years old) uses smokeless tobacco, and 1 in 10 young adults (18–25 years old) smokes cigars. The concurrent use of multiple tobacco products is common, too, with over 50% of white and Hispanic male tobacco users reporting that they use more than one tobacco product. The numbers are staggering. They translate into over a million new tobacco users a year in the United States alone. But there are proven methods to prevent this epidemic from claiming yet another generation, if our nation has the will to implement those methods in every state and community.

Nearly all tobacco use begins in childhood and adolescence. In all, 88% of adult cigarette smokers who smoke daily, report that they started smoking by the age of 18. This is a time in life of great vulnerability to social influences, and the pervasive presence of tobacco product marketing—including everything from sleek ads in magazines to youth-generated posts on social networking sites, to images of smoking in the movies—conveys messages that make tobacco use attractive to youth and young adults.

The first comprehensive surgeon general's report on youth, "Preventing Tobacco Use Among Young People," was published in 1994. That report concluded that if young people can remain free of tobacco until age 18, most will never start to smoke. The report documented the addiction process for young people and how the symptoms of addiction in youth are similar to those in adults. Use of tobacco was also presented as a gateway drug among young people, because its use generally precedes and increases the risk of illicit drug use. Cigarette advertising and promotional activities were seen as a potent way to increase the risk of cigarette smoking among young people, while community-wide efforts were shown to have been successful in reducing tobacco use among youth. All of these conclusions remain important, relevant, and accurate, as documented in the current report, but there has been considerable research since 1994 that greatly expands our knowledge about tobacco use among youth, its prevention, and the dynamics of cessation among young people. . . .

The Health Consequences of Tobacco Use Among Young People

While the 1994 surgeon general's report clearly identified that smoking had immediate and long-term health consequences for young people, further evidence . . . has strengthened these conclusions. Research now documents strong causal associations between active cigarette smoking in young people and addiction to nicotine, reduced lung function, reduced lung growth, asthma, and early abdominal aortic atherosclerosis. These associations have met the criteria for causality first introduced in the 1964 surgeon general's report: consistency, strength, specificity, temporality, and biological plausibility of the scientific evidence. These are serious social, physical, and mental health problems that manifest during adolescence and young adulthood and are the precursors to other long-term chronic diseases. Smoking is the chief preventable cause of premature death in this country, and the early stages of the diseases associated with adult smoking are already evident among young smokers. For example, young adult smokers under age 30 exhibit signs of and are being diagnosed with early disease of the abdominal aorta, a serious indicator of heart disease. . . . [And while] there is ample evidence that young people believe that cigarette smoking will help them control their body weight, there is no evidence that young smokers weigh less or lose weight because of their smoking. . . .

The Epidemiology of Tobacco Use Among Young People in the United States and Worldwide

The major national data sets that assess youth and young adult smoking were analyzed to provide updated data. . . . Cigarette smoking is shown, again, to primarily begin in adolescence, and very few adults begin to smoke after age 26 (1%). Since the 1994 surgeon general's report, tobacco use among adolescents and young adults has substantially decreased, especially since 1998. However, there has been a leveling off in the past few years, particularly since 2007, and in some groups there are increases in the prevalence of tobacco use, such as smokeless tobacco use among white males. Some groups of young people continue to smoke more than others, notably American Indians and Alaska Natives, but also whites and Hispanics. With the introduction of new tobacco products and promotion of smokeless tobacco products, use of multiple tobacco products is common. Among tobacco users, more than one-half of white and Hispanic high school males and almost one-half of Hispanic high school females use more than one product. . . .

Social, Environmental, Cognitive, and Genetic Influences on the Use of Tobacco Among Youth

Adolescents and young adults are uniquely vulnerable to influences to use tobacco. As young people move toward adulthood, they increasingly rely on their social contexts and peer groups in adopting or changing behavior. . . . Young people are more likely to use tobacco if their peers use tobacco or are antisocial. Those with higher academic achievement are less likely to use tobacco. Because of the particular vulnerability of this age group to peer group influences, external messages that target the peer group can be especially potent. . . .

The Tobacco Industry's Influences on the Use of Tobacco Among Youth

The tobacco companies spent nearly $10 billion in 2008 on advertising and promotional efforts. While there have been restrictions on marketing to young people as a result of the Master Settlement Agreement, there have not been corresponding reductions in marketing expenses—these have increased since 1998. Most tobacco industry marketing efforts involve promotional activities that reduce the price of cigarettes, strategies that should be effective with price-sensitive adolescents. Since the 1994 surgeon general's report, considerable evidence has accumulated that supports a causal association between marketing efforts of tobacco companies and the initiation and progression of tobacco use among young people. This evidence includes data from cross-sectional studies on exposure to advertising and use of tobacco; longitudinal studies with non-susceptible, never-users of tobacco and subsequent initiation; examination of industry marketing efforts

The State of Smoking in the United States

- Cigarette smoking, which is the most common form of tobacco use, causes approximately 443,000 deaths and costs about $96 billion in medical expenditures and $97 billion in productivity losses in the U.S. each year.

- After 40 years of steadily declining smoking rates, the decline in adult smoking rates in the U.S. has stalled. Currently about 1 in 5 adults smoke. Smoking is more common among people who live in poverty, live with mental illness or substance abuse disorders, have less than a high school education, or work at jobs that consist primarily of physical labor.

National Prevention Council, "National Prevention Strategy: America's Plan for Better Health and Wellness," US Department of Health and Human Services, Office of the Surgeon General, 2011, p. 28.

and use of specific brands; and evidence from tobacco industry documents on their marketing practices. This body of evidence consistently and coherently points to the intentional marketing of tobacco products to youth as being a cause of young people's tobacco use. The tobacco companies have launched antismoking efforts themselves, but while these efforts have had a positive impact on public perceptions of the tobacco industry among youth and young adults, they have not demonstrated success in impacting young people's tobacco use. Importantly, new avenues for restrictions on tobacco companies are now available and can be considered, such as changes in packaging, labeling, product design, and restricting smoking in movies. . . .

A Vision for Ending the Tobacco Epidemic

Public health programs and policies have been in effect since the 19th century to dissuade young people from using tobacco. The first surgeon general's report in 1964 provided irrefutable evidence of the harmful consequences of smoking and yet, 15 years later, as noted in the 1979 surgeon general's report, rates of smoking among young people had not changed. By 1994, when the first surgeon general's report focused on youth was released, smoking rates among young people were increasing, despite 30 years of evidence that cigarette smoking had become the leading cause of death in the United States. Since that landmark 1994 report, a large body of research, litigation by individual states and the federal government, the Master Settlement Agreement, and authority granted to the FDA [US Food and Drug Administration] have substantially changed the tobacco control policy environment, and tobacco advertising and promotional activities have been somewhat curtailed. The rates of tobacco use among youth and young adults began to decrease from the late 1990s to the mid-2000s. Thus, progress in reducing tobacco use has been achieved, but there still remain significant challenges ahead. Nearly one-fourth of our high school seniors are current smokers, and the decreasing rates of tobacco use have leveled off, and in some subgroups have increased since 2007. The efforts of the early 21st century need to be reinvigorated, and additional strategies considered, to end the tobacco epidemic. Providing and sustaining sufficient funding for comprehensive community programs, statewide tobacco control programs, school-based policies and programs, and mass media campaigns must be a priority. Taxing tobacco products is especially effective in reducing their use among young people. Greater consideration of further restrictions on advertising and promotional activities, as well as efforts to decrease depictions of smoking in the movies, is warranted, given the gravity of the epidemic and the need to protect young people now and in the future.

> "In 2010, the total number of cigarettes sold and given away declined again, to 281.6 billion units."

Tobacco Sales Are Declining

Federal Trade Commission

In the following viewpoint, the Federal Trade Commission (FTC) reports that tobacco sales and marketing are decreasing. According to the commission, the total number of cigarettes sold or given away by tobacco companies decreased by billions during the past few years, down 32.3 billion (10 percent) from 2008 to 2009 and an additional 8.6 billion (3 percent) in 2010. In addition, the FTC states that advertising and promotional expenditures have also decreased in general, from $9.94 billion in 2008 to $8.53 billion in 2009 to $8.05 billion in 2010. Established in 1914, the FTC is a bipartisan federal agency dedicated to protecting American consumers and promoting competition.

As you read, consider the following questions:

1. What figures does the FTC provide for declining cigarette sales between 2008 and 2009?

2. As claimed by the FTC, what is "sampling"?

3. How have the sales of cigarettes with tar ratings of fifteen milligrams and three milligrams changed from 2009 to 2010, as described by the FTC?

"Cigarette Report for 2009 and 2010," Federal Trade Commission, 2012, pp. 1–8.

The total number of cigarettes reported sold or given away by the major manufacturers decreased by 32.3 billion cigarettes (10.0 percent) from 2008 to 2009, and then by another 8.6 billion units (3.0 percent) from 2009 to 2010. Advertising and promotional expenditures also declined, falling from $9.94 billion in 2008 to $8.53 billion in 2009, and then to $8.05 billion in 2010. The largest single category of these expenditures in both 2009 and 2010 was price discounts paid to cigarette retailers or wholesalers in order to reduce the price of cigarettes to consumers. This one category accounted for $6.67 billion (78.2 percent of total advertising and promotional expenditures) in 2009, and $6.49 billion (80.7 percent of total expenditures) in 2010. . . .

Cigarettes Sold and Given Away

In 2009, the five major domestic cigarette manufacturers sold or gave away 290.3 billion cigarettes domestically, down from 322.6 billion in 2008. Sales declined from 320.0 billion in 2008 to 290.2 billion in 2009, while cigarettes given away declined from 2.7 billion in 2008 to 0.1 billion in 2009. In 2010, the total number of cigarettes sold and given away declined again, to 281.6 billion units. . . .

Because the major manufacturers report sales data to the [Federal Trade] Commission based on factory shipments, which can reflect changes in inventory holdings by cigarette wholesalers and retailers, the commission's reports for a number of years included data produced by the U.S. Department of Agriculture (USDA), which were based on an estimate of the number of cigarettes actually consumed. USDA data are not available for years after 2006. . . .

Advertising and Promotional Expenditures by Category

Overall, $8.53 billion was spent on cigarette advertising and promotion in 2009, a decline from the $9.94 billion the major cigarette manufacturers reported in 2008. Total expenditures declined further, to $8.05 billion, in 2010.

The companies reported spending $36.7 million in 2009 on magazine advertising (up from $25.5 million in 2008) and $46.5 million in 2010.

Spending on "outdoor" advertising decreased from $2.0 million in 2008 to $1.8 million in 2009, and then to $1.7 million in 2010. Since 2002, "outdoor" advertising has been defined to mean billboards; signs and placards in arenas, stadiums, and shopping malls (whether they are open air or enclosed); and any other advertisements placed outdoors, regardless of their size, including those on cigarette retailer property. Before 2002, "outdoor" advertising was not precisely defined and it was not clear that signs in arenas, stadiums, shopping malls, or on retailer property would have been reported in this category.

As they have since 2001, the companies reported no expenditures on transit advertising (*i.e.*, advertising in or on private or public vehicles or any transportation facility) in 2009 or 2010.

Spending on point-of-sale promotional materials (ads posted at the retail location but excluding outdoor ads on retailer property) fell from $163.7 million in 2008 to $110.3 million in 2009, and then to $106.6 million in 2010.

The "Promotional Allowance" Category

Since 2002, the "promotional allowance" category has been replaced by four separate categories: price discounts, promotional allowances paid to retailers, promotional allowances paid to wholesalers, and other promotional allowances. For both 2009 and 2010, the largest "promotional allowance" category was price discounts paid to cigarette retailers or wholesalers in order to reduce the price of cigarettes to consumers (*e.g.*, off-invoice discounts, buy downs, and voluntary price reductions), which accounted for expenditures of $6.67 billion in 2009 (down from $7.17 billion in 2008) and $6.49 billion in 2010.

In addition, the industry spent $428.7 million in 2009 (down from $481.5 million in 2008) and $370.0 million in 2010 on promotional allowances paid to cigarette retailers in order to facilitate the sale or placement of cigarettes (*e.g.*, payments for stocking, shelving, displaying, and merchandising brands, volume rebates, and incentive payments); $449.0 million (2009) and $410.4 million (2010) on promotional allowances paid to cigarette wholesalers (*e.g.*, payments for volume rebates, incentive payments, value-added services, and promotional executions); and $965,000 (2009) and $210,000 (2010) on promotional allowances paid to persons other than retailers and wholesalers. When these four promotional allowance categories are combined, they total $7.55 billion, and account for 88.5 percent of all 2009 spending; for 2010, they total $7.27 billion, 90.4 percent of all spending.

Money spent giving cigarette samples to the public ("sampling distribution") decreased from $54.3 million in 2008 to $23.8 million in 2009, and then to $22.2 million in 2010. "Sampling" includes, among other things, when coupons are distributed for free cigarettes and no purchase is required. . . .

Advertisements to Reduce Youth Smoking

In 2001, the commission began requiring the manufacturers to report expenditures on advertisements directed to youth or their parents that are intended to reduce youth smoking. The companies reported spending $8.1 million on such advertising in 2009, and $4.4 million in 2010. The companies had previously reported spending $20.7 million and $11.5 million on such advertising in 2007 and 2008, respectively. These figures do not include contributions to third parties that engage in such programs.

Smoking Rates Have Declined

In the United States, smoking rates have declined since the surgeon general's warning in 1964. Between 1965 and 1999, the proportion of the U.S. adult population that smoked decreased from 42.4% to only 23.5%. Although the reduction in cigarette smoking over the last three decades has been much greater in men, the rate of current cigarette use remains higher in men (25.7%) than in women (21.5%).

Erich M. Sturgis and Qingyi Wei,
"Epidemiology of Oral Cancer," in Oral Cancer:
Diagnosis, Management, and Rehabilitation.
Ed. John W. Werning. New York:
Thieme Medical Publishing, 2011, p. 3.

Cigarette manufacturers reported that neither they nor anyone working for them nor on their behalf paid money or any other form of compensation in connection with the production or filming of any motion picture or television show in 2009 or 2010, or paid money or any other form of compensation to anyone engaged in product placement in motion pictures or television shows. The companies also reported that neither they nor anyone working for them nor on their behalf sought, solicited, granted approval, or otherwise gave permission for the appearance of any cigarette product or cigarette brand imagery in any motion picture, television show, or video appearing on the Internet, although one company reported having videos on company websites that were restricted to its employees, contractors, and retailers....

Tar Ratings, Filters, Length, and Flavor

In 2009, cigarettes with tar ratings of 15 mg [milligrams] or less constituted 82.3 percent of the domestic cigarette market, while cigarettes with tar ratings of 3 mg or less—the lowest rated portion of the market—made up 0.4 percent of the market. In 2010, these figures were 91.3 percent and 0.4 percent, respectively. . . .

Filtered cigarettes have dominated the market since the commission began collecting this information in 1963. Filtered cigarettes accounted for 99.5 percent of the market in both 2009 and 2010. . . .

The king-size (79–88 mm [millimeter]) category continues to be the biggest seller, with 64 percent of the market in 2009 and 62 percent in 2010. This category is followed by the long (94–101 mm) group, which held 32 percent of the market in 2009 and 33 percent in 2010. The shortest category (68–72 mm) rose to 4 percent of the total market in 2010; the last time these cigarettes held more than 2 percent of the market was 1985. . . .

In 2008, menthol cigarettes were 27 percent of the market, while non-menthols held 73 percent of the market. In 2009, those percentages were 21 percent and 79 percent, respectively; in 2010, menthol cigarettes were 22 percent of the market.

| "*Each day, nearly 4,000 kids under the age of 18 try their first cigarette and another 1,000 become regular, daily smokers.*"

Teen Smoking Is a Serious Problem

American Cancer Society

Founded in 1913, the American Cancer Society (ACS) is a na-tionwide voluntary health organization focused on cancer as a public health issue. In the following viewpoint, the ACS asserts that tobacco use among children and teens is a serious issue. The number of young Americans who smoke has been decreasing since the 1990s, but each day about four thousand youths under eighteen years old try their first cigarette, and one thousand more pick up a regular habit, explains the ACS. Furthermore, the organization adds that more than 23 percent of high school students have used a form of tobacco in the past month, selecting from flavored cigars, electronic cigarettes, and other products. What is crucial is that virtually all smokers start by the age of twenty-six, with nine out of ten first smoking by age eighteen, the ACS claims.

As you read, consider the following questions:

1. According to the ACS, what do teen smokers say about quitting?

2. Why will the problem of youths smoking small cigars get even worse, in the words of the ACS?

3. What figures does the ACS cite for the use of electronic cigarettes among middle school students?

The good news: The number of younger Americans who smoke cigarettes has been going down since the late 1990s.

The bad news: Each day, nearly 4,000 kids under the age of 18 try their first cigarette and another 1,000 become regular, daily smokers. About one-third of these smokers will die prematurely from a smoking-related disease.

More bad news: As of 2012, more than 23% of all high school students (grades 9–12) had used some kind of tobacco product in the past month. Now, there are many more forms of tobacco to choose from, and more teens are choosing flavored cigars, smokeless tobacco, hookahs, pipes, and even electronic cigarettes. Some still smoke cigarettes.

Whatever they choose, kids are getting hooked in high school—by 12th grade, about half the smokers had tried to quit at least once in the past year.

Children and teens are easy targets for the tobacco industry. They're often influenced by TV, movies, the Internet, advertising, and by what their friends do and say. They don't realize what a struggle it can be to quit. And having cancer, emphysema, blindness, or impotence may not seem like real concerns—kids and teens don't think much about future health outcomes. . . .

Facts About Kids and Tobacco

Almost all smokers start while they're young

In 2012, 18% of high school girls and 23% of high school boys used some form of tobacco at least one day in the month before the survey. Studies have found that nearly all first use of tobacco takes place before high school graduation.

According to the 2012 surgeon general's report, very few people start smoking after age 25: 99% of adult smokers first smoked by age 26. Nearly 9 out of 10 adult smokers had their first smoke by age 18.

The younger a person is when they start using tobacco, the more likely they are to use it as an adult. And people who start regularly using tobacco when they are younger are more likely to have trouble quitting than people who start later in life.

This means if we can keep kids tobacco free until age 18, most will never start using it.

Kids who smoke have smoking-related health problems

Cigarette smoking causes serious health problems in children and teens. Children and teens who smoke regularly have problems such as:

- Coughing spells

- Shortness of breath, even when not exercising

- Wheezing or gasping

- More frequent headaches

- Increased phlegm (mucus)

- Respiratory illnesses that are worse and happen more often

- Worse cold and flu symptoms

- Reduced physical fitness

- Poor lung growth and function

- Worse overall health

- Addiction to nicotine

As they get older, teens who continue to smoke can expect problems like:

- Gum disease and tooth loss

- Infertility and impotence

- Chronic lung diseases, like emphysema and bronchitis, which limit exercise and activity

- Hearing loss

- Vision problems, such as macular degeneration, which can lead to blindness

- Blood vessel disease, which can lead to heart attacks or strokes at a young age

Most young smokers are addicted and find it hard to quit

Most young people who smoke regularly are already addicted to nicotine. In fact, they have the same kind of addiction as adult smokers. According to the 2012 surgeon general's report:

"Of every three young smokers, only one will quit, and one of those remaining smokers will die from tobacco-related causes. Most of these young people never considered the long-term health consequences associated with tobacco use when they started smoking; and nicotine, a highly addictive drug, causes many to continue smoking well into adulthood, often with deadly consequences."

Most teen smokers say that they would like to quit and many have tried to do so without success. Those who try to quit smoking report withdrawal symptoms much like those reported by adults.

Tobacco use is linked to other harmful behaviors

Research has shown that teen tobacco users are more likely to use alcohol and illegal drugs than are nonusers. Cigarette smokers are also more likely to get into fights, carry weapons, attempt suicide, suffer from mental health problems such as depression, and engage in high-risk sexual behaviors.

Look at the Numbers

Tobacco use in middle school students

The most recent numbers on tobacco use among US middle school students come from a 2012 survey by the CDC [Centers for Disease Control and Prevention]. (Middle school includes children in grades 6, 7, and 8.)

- Nearly 7% of middle school students reported using some form of tobacco—cigarettes, spit or other oral tobacco, cigars, hookahs, pipes, electronic cigarettes (e-cigarettes), and flavored cigarettes like bidis or kreteks—at least once in the past 30 days.

- 3.5% of the students had smoked cigarettes, and 2.8% had smoked cigars. Nearly 2% had smoked pipes, 1.3% had smoked hookahs, and 1.1% had used e-cigarettes. Around 0.5% had used kreteks and about the same number had smoked bidis (0.6%).

- 1.7% used spit or other smokeless tobacco. Nearly 1% had used snus (a newer form of snuff). Half a percent (0.5%) had used dissolvable tobacco.

- Boys (about 8%) were more likely than girls (about 6%) to use some form of tobacco.

Tobacco use in high school students

The most recent tobacco numbers for high school students come from the 2012 CDC youth tobacco survey and other CDC surveys. Keep in mind that these studies are done with students who are still in school. Those who drop out have higher rates of smoking and tobacco use, and are not included in these numbers.

- Nationwide, more than 23% of high school students reported using some type of tobacco (cigarette, cigar, pipe, bidi, kretek, hookah, e-cigarette, or some form of smokeless tobacco) on at least 1 of the 30 days before the survey.

- On average, about 1 out of 7 students (14%) smoked cigarettes. Girls (12%) were less likely to smoke cigarettes than boys (16%). White students (15%) were more likely to smoke cigarettes than black (10%), or Hispanic/Latino (14%) students.

- About 13% of high school students had smoked cigars in the last 30 days. Male students (17%) were more likely to smoke cigars than female students (8%).

- About 6% of high school students reported using spit or other smokeless tobacco at least once in the 30 days before the survey. About 11% of all the boys and about 2% of all the girls surveyed had used smokeless tobacco.

- About half of all the school students who reported that they still smoked had tried to quit at least once during the year before.

- Other tobacco use among high school students included pipes (over 4%), bidis (about 1%), and kreteks (about 1%).

Other Forms of Tobacco Favored by Young People

Cigars: Cigars are often thought to be less harmful, less addictive, and more stylish than cigarettes—though this is not true.

Since 1998, small cigars have been the fastest-growing product on the cigar market. Many of the smaller cigars look much the same as cigarettes except for their color (they're brown, not white), and are also sold in packs.

Another appeal to youth is the flavorings commonly used in small cigars. Fruit, candy, and chocolate flavors attract kids. US laws have made flavored cigarettes illegal, which seems to have prompted some to use flavored small cigars instead. It's expected that the small and flavored cigar problem will get even worse as tobacco companies take advantage of the lack of regulation of these products.

Because they're cigars, most of them are not taxed as much or regulated the way cigarettes are. This makes them cheaper and easier for kids to get, too.

Cigars are just as addictive and deadly as cigarettes. The smaller ones are often inhaled and smoked every day, just like cigarettes. Even when cigar smoke is not inhaled, smokers are breathing cigar smoke from the air around them. It's no wonder that cigars cause many of the same types of cancer and other illnesses as cigarettes. . . .

Spit or smokeless tobacco use among kids: Spit or smokeless tobacco is a less lethal, but still unsafe, alternative to smoking. Many terms are used to describe tobacco that is put into the mouth, such as spit, spitless, oral tobacco, and chewing or snuff tobacco.

The use of spit or smokeless tobacco by any name can cause:

- Cancers of the mouth

- Cancers of the pharynx (throat) and larynx (voice box)

- Cancers of the esophagus (swallowing tube) and stomach

- Cancer of the pancreas

- Receding gums and gum disease, which can worsen to the point that the teeth fall out

- Pre-cancerous spots in the mouth, called leukoplakia (loo-ko-PLAY-key-uh)

- Nicotine addiction

There is also a link to heart disease and stroke. And research has shown that teens who use spit or other oral tobacco are more likely to become smokers than nonusers.

Snus and dissolvable tobacco: Snus and dissolvable tobacco are two new forms of smokeless tobacco that are now being used by kids and teens.

Snus (pronounced "snoose") is a finely ground form of moist snuff made of tobacco and flavorings. Snus is often packaged in small pouches, but can also be used like loose moist snuff. In the 2012 survey, 2.5% of high school students had used snus in the past month.

Dissolvables are sold as lozenges, tablets (orbs or pellets), strips, and sticks that contain tobacco and nicotine. Depending on the type, they are held in the mouth, chewed, or sucked until they are absorbed by the tissues of the mouth. Some of these products are mint flavored and look like candy. Others look like toothpicks or melt-away mouthwash strips. In 2012, about 1% of high school students had recently used them. . . .

Smokeless tobacco is promoted where smoking is banned. Unfortunately, tobacco companies have used the smoking bans in many states to push for people to use spit and other smokeless tobacco. As recommended by the Centers for Disease Control and Prevention (CDC), many schools no longer allow students, staff, parents, or visitors to smoke on school grounds, in school vehicles, or at school functions. Many workplaces are making changes like this, too. Tobacco companies have quickly stepped in to market their smokeless products. Many of these new tobacco products are being advertised as more discreet alternatives to smoking in places where smoking is not allowed. . . .

Some companies promote using spit or smokeless tobacco as a way to help quit smoking, but there's no proof that spit tobacco or any other oral tobacco products help smokers quit smoking. Unlike US Food and Drug Administration (FDA)–approved standard treatments that have been proven to work (such as nicotine replacement, specific types of antidepressants, nicotine receptor blockers, and behavioral therapy), oral tobacco products have not been tested to see if they can help a person stop smoking.

Hookahs (water pipes): Hookah is also called *narghile* (nar-guh-lee) *smoking*. It started in Asia and the Middle East. It involves burning tobacco that has been mixed with flavors such as honey, molasses, or fruit in a water pipe and inhaling the flavored smoke through a long hose. Usually, the tobacco mixture, which is called *shisha* (she-shuh), is heated using charcoal. Hookah smoking is often a social event which allows the smokers to spend time together and talk as they pass the pipe around.

Hookah smoking has become popular among younger people in Western countries. More than 5% of high school students surveyed in 2012 had used a hookah in the past month. For young people, hookahs are a popular and socially acceptable way to smoke tobacco.

Hookahs are marketed as being a safe alternative to cigarettes. This claim is false. The water does not filter out the toxins. In fact, hookah smoke has been shown to contain concentrations of toxins, such as carbon monoxide, nicotine, tar, and heavy metals, that are as high, or higher, than those that are seen with cigarette smoke. And people tested after hookah smoking have been found to have higher levels of carbon monoxide in their blood than those who had smoked a cigarette.

Several types of cancer, including lung cancer, have been linked to hookah smoking. Hookah is also linked to other unique risks not associated with cigarette smoking. For example, infectious diseases including tuberculosis (which can infect the lungs or other parts of the body), aspergillus (a fungus that can cause serious lung infections), and helicobacter (which can cause stomach ulcers), or even Epstein-Barr virus (EBV, which can cause mononucleosis and is linked to a few types of cancer) may be spread by sharing the pipe or through the way the tobacco is prepared.

Newer forms of hookah smoking can include steam stones or even battery-powered hookah pens. Both of these create a vapor that is inhaled, which makes them more like electronic cigarettes. Some advertise that they are purer and healthier alternatives to regular hookahs, even though less is known about them.

Electronic cigarettes: Electronic cigarettes are small refillable devices that look like cigarettes. They use battery power to vaporize nicotine solutions so they can be inhaled. The vapor can be flavored like fruit and candy, which appeals to youth. As of late 2013, there are no national restrictions on the sale of these products to children, although many states forbid sales to minors.

Among middle school students, those who had ever used e-cigarettes nearly doubled from 1.4% to 2.7% during 2011–2012. Students reporting e-cigarette use in the month before the survey climbed from 0.6% to 1.1%. As of 2012, 0.7% used both e-cigarettes and conventional cigarettes.

High school students who reported ever using e-cigarettes more than doubled, from 4.7% to 10.0% during 2011–2012. Students reporting e-cigarette use in the past month increased from 1.5% to 2.8%. As of 2012, 2.2% used both cigarettes and e-cigarettes, although some students used only e-cigarettes.

Kreteks and bidis: Clove and other flavored cigarettes are used mostly by younger smokers. They are nearly ideal in design as a "trainer cigarette"—giving kids another way to experiment with tobacco and get addicted to nicotine. The false image of these products as clean, natural, and safer than regular cigarettes seems to attract some young people who might otherwise not start smoking. But they are not safer than cigarettes, and each has its own additional problems.

New federal laws banned flavored cigarettes as of October 2009; it's still legal to have or smoke them, but it's illegal to sell them in the US. They can sometimes be found in online shops hosted from other countries, even though the US FDA has warned both foreign and domestic websites that flavored cigarettes can't be sold here. US tobacco companies are working around this ban by making flavored small cigars as a replacement product. . . .

Clove cigarettes, also called kreteks (kree-teks), are a tobacco product with the same health risks as cigarettes. Kreteks contain 60% to 70% tobacco and 30% to 40% ground cloves, clove oil, and other additives. They deliver more nicotine, carbon monoxide, and tar than regular cigarettes. They mainly come from Indonesia and other Southeast Asian countries, although there is information on the Internet on how to make your own.

Kretek smokers have higher risks of asthma and other lung diseases than nonsmokers. Kreteks can cause lung problems right away, such as lower oxygen levels, fluid in the lungs, and inflammation. Regular kretek smokers have up to 20 times the risk for abnormal lung function (blocked airways or poor oxygen uptake) compared with nonsmokers. But kretek users often have the mistaken notion that smoking clove cigarettes is a safe alternative to smoking tobacco—this is not true. Laws against flavored cigarettes also apply to kreteks, and the FDA has warned companies that they can't be sold in the United States. . . .

Flavored cigarettes, called *bidis* or *beedies*, often come from India and other Southeast Asian countries. They have become popular with young people in the United States. This is in part because they are sold in candy-like flavors such as chocolate, cherry, strawberry, licorice, and orange. Some people think they are safer and more natural than regular cigarettes. They tend to cost less than regular cigarettes and they give the smoker a quick buzz due to the high levels of nicotine.

Bidis are tobacco hand-rolled in a tendu or temburni leaf (plants native to Asia) and tied with colorful strings on the ends. Even though bidis contain less tobacco than regular cigarettes, they deliver 3 to 5 times more nicotine than regular cigarettes. They are unfiltered. And because they are thinner than regular cigarettes, they require about 3 times as many puffs per cigarette.

Bidis appear to have all of the same health risks of regular cigarettes, if not more. Bidi smokers have much higher risks of heart attacks, heart disease, emphysema, chronic bronchitis, and some cancers than nonsmokers.

"*Since the peak year in 1997, the proportion of students currently smoking has dropped by two-thirds—an extremely important development for the health and longevity of this generation of Americans.*"

Teen Smoking Is Declining

L.D. Johnston, P.M. O'Malley, J.G. Bachman, and J.E. Schulenberg

L.D. Johnston, P.M. O'Malley, J.G. Bachman, and J.E. Schulenberg are research professors at the University of Michigan's Institute for Social Research, which conducts Monitoring the Future (MTF) surveys that investigate youth substance abuse each year. In the following viewpoint, the authors claim that smoking is in decline among teens in grades eight, ten, and twelve. For all three grades, the percentage of students that reported smoking in the last thirty days decreased from 10.6 percent to 9.6 percent, according to MTF's 2013 survey. Reflecting a one-tenth decrease, the survey shows that this follows a similar decrease from the previous year, eventually preventing thousands of premature deaths and tobacco-related illnesses. As for other forms of tobacco, such as hookah and snus, teen use has either modestly declined or leveled off after rising, conclude the authors.

L.D. Johnston, P.M. O'Malley, J.G. Bachman, and J.E. Schulenberg, National press release, "Teen Smoking Continues to Decline in 2013," December 18, 2013. University of Michigan News Service, Ann Arbor.

As you read, consider the following questions:

1. According to the viewpoint, what does Lloyd Johnston state about longer term declines in teen smoking?

2. What is the authors' finding in 2013 on teens who personally disapprove of smoking?

3. What figures do the authors provide to support their assertion that the use of snus is abating after making inroads among twelfth graders?

Smoking among teens in grades 8, 10 and 12 continued to decline in 2013—a positive trend since most smokers begin their habit in adolescence—according to the latest survey results from the nationwide Monitoring the Future study.

Based on annual surveys of 40,000 to 50,000 students in about 400 secondary schools, the researchers found that the percentage of students saying that they smoked at all in the prior 30 days fell for the three grades combined, from 10.6 percent to 9.6 percent—a statistically significant drop.

"This year's decline means that the number of youngsters actively smoking has dropped by almost one-tenth over just the past year, and it follows a decline of about the same magnitude last year," said Lloyd Johnston, the principal investigator of the study. "Since the peak year in 1997, the proportion of students currently smoking has dropped by two-thirds—an extremely important development for the health and longevity of this generation of Americans."

Such a reduction can translate eventually into preventing thousands of premature deaths as well as tens of thousands of serious diseases, he said. More than 400,000 Americans per year are estimated to die prematurely as a result of smoking cigarettes.

An increase in the federal tax on tobacco products, instituted in 2009, may have contributed to the recent declines in smoking in this age group, according to the investigators.

The Monitoring the Future study, which has been tracking teen smoking in the United States for nearly four decades, found that between 2012 and 2013 the percentage of students reporting any cigarette smoking in the prior 30 days (called 30-day prevalence) has decreased among 8th graders from 4.9 percent to 4.5 percent, among 10th graders from 10.8 percent to 9.1 percent, and among 12th graders from 17.1 percent to 16.3 percent (the decline in 30-day prevalence between 2012 and 2013 is statistically significant for 10th graders and for all three grades combined; longer term declines . . . across the past five years are highly statistically significant in all grades.)

"While the improvements in the smoking numbers for just this one year are important, of course, the longer term declines are much more so," Johnston said. "Since teen smoking reached a peak around 1996–1997, the rates of current (past 30-day) smoking have fallen by nearly 80 percent among 8th graders, 70 percent among 10th graders and over 50 percent among 12th graders. Further, the proportional declines in *daily* smoking are even larger."

One important cause of these declines in current smoking is that fewer young people today have ever started to smoke. In 1996, 49 percent of 8th graders said they had tried cigarettes, but by 2013 only 15 percent said they had done so—a drop of seven-tenths in smoking initiation over the past 17 years. Further, the initiation of smoking continues to fall significantly among students.

These estimates come from the study's national surveys of students in about 400 secondary schools each year. The study was designed and is directed by a team of research professors at the University of Michigan's Institute for Social Research, and since its inception has been funded through research grants from the National Institute on Drug Abuse—one of the National Institutes of Health.

Attitudes and Beliefs About Smoking

Perceived Availability. Students in 8th and 10th grades are asked how difficult they think it would be for them to get cigarettes, if they wanted them. This *perceived availability* has shown a substantial decline since 1996, one that has continued into 2013. The 8th graders have shown the sharpest decline—from 77 percent saying they could get cigarettes "fairly easily" or "very easily" in 1996 to 50 percent today. Perceived availability among 10th graders fell from about 90 percent to 70 percent over the same interval.

"Although some real progress has been made in reducing the availability of cigarettes to those who are underage—particularly to the youngest teens—it is clear that the majority of teens still think they can get cigarettes fairly easily," Johnston said.

Attitudes and Beliefs About Smoking. Nearly two-thirds of 8th graders and about three-quarters of 10th and 12th graders said they see a great risk of harm to the user from pack-a-day smoking. These figures have increased substantially since the mid-1990s, when perceived risk was at its recent lowest levels. The 2012 figures were the highest ever recorded for all three grade levels; however, perceived risk did not continue to rise in 2013. The percentages of teens saying that they personally *disapprove* of smoking were also at the highest levels seen in this study in 2012—89 percent, 86 percent and 84 percent for grades 8, 10 and 12, respectively—but this attitude has shown no further increase in 2013 either.

Other attitudes toward smoking and smokers have changed in important ways, especially during much of the period of decline in cigarette use. These changes include increases in preferring to date nonsmokers (currently around 78 percent of teens report this preference, down very slightly from last year), strongly disliking being around people who are smoking, thinking that becoming a smoker reflects poor judgment, and believing that smoking is a dirty habit. All of these negative attitudes about smoking and smokers rose to high levels by 2007, but they have either leveled or begun to reverse since then.

"The halt in the increases in perceived risk and disapproval of smoking are not good signs, nor is the softening in other attitudes related to smoking," Johnston said. "As a result, future progress in lowering teen smoking rates is likely to depend on there being further changes in the external environment—such as raising cigarette taxes, further limiting where smoking is permitted, bringing back broad-based anti-smoking ad campaigns, and making quit-smoking programs more available."

Other Tobacco Products

At the same time that cigarette smoking has been receding among young people, a number of other forms of tobacco consumption are being introduced into the market. Public health professionals worry that, with aggressive marketing and fewer federal controls, these other forms of tobacco consumption will begin to offset the hard-won gains in cigarette smoking.

Smokeless Tobacco. The use of smokeless tobacco (which includes snuff, plug, dipping tobacco, chewing tobacco, and more recently, "snus") also is assessed in the study ("snus" is singular and rhymes with "goose"). From the mid-1990s to the early 2000s, there was a substantial decline in the use of smokeless tobacco among teens—30-day prevalence fell by one-third to one-half in all grades—but the declines ended and a rebound in use developed from the mid-2000s through 2010.

After 2010, however, there were modest declines in all three grades for a couple of years, although they did not continue into 2013 (none of the changes for smokeless tobacco use in 2013 is statistically significant at any grade level). Thirty-day prevalence rates are now down by nearly two-

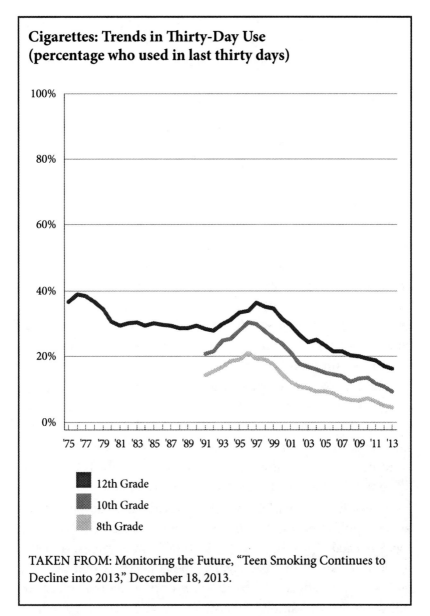

Cigarettes: Trends in Thirty-Day Use (percentage who used in last thirty days)

Legend:
- 12th Grade
- 10th Grade
- 8th Grade

TAKEN FROM: Monitoring the Future, "Teen Smoking Continues to Decline into 2013," December 18, 2013.

thirds (63 percent) from their peaks in the mid-1990s among 8th graders, and by nearly four-tenths among 10th graders and one-third among 12th graders. Thirty-day prevalence rates for smokeless tobacco use in 2013 are 2.8 percent, 6.4 percent and 8.1 percent among 8th, 10th and 12th graders, respectively. The rates in each of the three grades are considerably higher for boys (3.8 percent, 11.1 percent and 14.6 percent) than for girls (1.9 percent, 2.0 percent and 1.4 percent).

Perceived risk, which MTF [Monitoring the Future] has shown to be an important determinant of trends for many forms of substance use, including cigarette use, also appears to have played an important role in the decline of smokeless tobacco use. In all three grades, perceived risk for smokeless tobacco rose fairly steadily from 1995 through 2004, as use was falling.

However, there was not a great deal of falloff in perceived risk subsequently, between 2004 and 2010, suggesting that other factors may have led to the increases in smokeless tobacco use in that time interval. These factors might include increased promotion of these products, a proliferation of types of smokeless tobacco products available and increased restrictions on places where cigarette smoking is permitted.

The leveling in smokeless use since 2010 may be attributable, at least in part, to the 2009 increase in federal taxes on tobacco. However, perceived risk for smokeless tobacco declined significantly in 2012 in the lower grades and has fallen again in 2013—this time in all three grades—which the investigators believe could portend a future rise in use.

Hookahs and Small Cigars. Two of the latest developments to raise public health concern are the smoking of tobacco by using hookah (pronounced "WHO-ka") water pipes, and the smoking of small or little cigars. The concern is that as cigarette smoking continues to decline among adolescents, they will be enticed to smoke tobacco in these other forms, which still carry serious health risks.

Questions about these forms of tobacco use in the prior 12 months (annual prevalence) were included in the survey of 12th graders for the first time in 2010, when 17.1 percent of 12th graders said that they had used a hookah to smoke tobacco in the prior 12 months. This rate has risen to 21.4 percent by 2013, including a significant 3.1 percentage-point increase in 2013. Only about 9 percent of 12th-grade students in 2013 reported smoking with a hookah more than five times during the year, suggesting a considerable amount of light or experimental use. Males had only a slightly higher annual prevalence rate than females—22 percent versus 21 percent.

Smoking small cigars is about as prevalent a behavior as hookah smoking, with 12th graders having an annual prevalence of 20 percent in 2013. This is unchanged from 2011 and 2012 and is lower than the first reading on these products in 2010 (23 percent). Only 12 percent of 12th-grade students in 2012 or 2013 indicate use on more than two occasions during the year, and only 2 percent indicate using them more than 20 times. There is a larger gender difference for this form of tobacco use than for hookah smoking, with an annual prevalence of 27 percent among male 12th graders compared to 15 percent among females.

"We are continuing to monitor these two forms of tobacco consumption to see if they represent a growing problem among youth, and we will be examining their use among young adults, as well," Johnston said.

One important development is that some manufacturers have slightly raised the weight of their small cigars in order to remove them from FDA oversight under current law, he said. A number are flavored, for example, which is likely to make them more attractive to young people. And the slight rise in weight substantially lowers the federal tax.

Snus and Dissolvable Tobacco. In 2011, questions were introduced dealing with two more recent forms of tobacco use— snus and dissolvable tobacco. The question about snus—a moist form of snuff that is placed under the upper lip—asks on how many occasions in the past 12 months the student ". . . used snus (a small packet of tobacco that is put in the mouth)." Among 12th graders in 2011, 7.9 percent reported having used snus in the last 12 months—a rate that remained essentially unchanged in 2012 (7.9 percent) and 2013 (7.7 percent). The proportion using more than two times is 5.3 percent in both 2012 and 2013.

Clearly, snus has made some inroads among 12th graders, but that seems to be abating, Johnston said. In 2012, the question about use of snus was added to the questionnaires administered to 8th and 10th graders, and in 2013 a significant decline in use is evident among 10th graders (down 1.7 percentage points to 5.2 percent). The pattern of use by subgroups of 12th-grade students follows the pattern for all smokeless products generally, with use much higher among males (14.6 percent versus 1.4 percent among females).

The question about dissolvable tobacco products asks on how many occasions in the past 12 months the student "... used dissolvable tobacco products." These products, in the form of pellets, strips or sticks, actually dissolve in the mouth, unlike other forms of chewing tobacco. Among 12th graders in 2011, only 1.5 percent reported having used in the prior 12 months. In 2012, it was 1.6 percent, and in 2013 it was 1.9 percent. Since the question was introduced for the lower grades in 2012, the annual prevalence rates in 2013 show little change, currently at 1.1 percent for grade 8 and 1.2 percent for grade 10. It appears that these products have not yet made significant inroads among secondary school students.

| "Secondhand smoke is anything but second in nature."

Secondhand Smoke Is Dangerous

Frances Robert Lato

A former smoker, Frances Robert Lato is author of Tobacco Road: How to Choose Not to Use. *In the following viewpoint excerpted from* Tobacco Road, *he argues that secondhand smoke is just as harmful as smoking. Nonsmokers in smoking environments take in multiple times more smoke than normal consumption, according to Lato, leading to lung cancer and health problems in people who do not smoke. Likewise, he claims that nonsmokers can actually become addicted to smoke and acquire the habits of smokers around them. Therefore, he strongly recommends that nonsmokers and smokers alike acknowledge the dangers of secondhand smoke and avoid exposure or exposing it to others by all means.*

As you read, consider the following questions:

1. Why does the author call secondhand smoke "used smoke"?

Frances Robert Lato, *Tobacco Road: How to Choose Not to Use,* Indianapolis, IN: Dog Ear Publishing, 2010, pp. 51–57. Copyright © 2014 Frances Robert Lato. All rights reserved. Reproduced with permission.

2. In the author's view, why does secondhand smoke affect smokers?

3. What example does Lato provide to back his claim that nonsmokers can become addicted to smoke?

Secondhand smoke. Let's call it what it really is. Used smoke.

Well, that is exactly what it is after all. I have read many articles over the years with respects to secondhand smoke and how restaurants were going smoke free and the precautions taken by other businesses as well. It is very clear that to breathe smoke from someone else's tobacco is just as bad for you as if you were breathing it directly. Studies have shown that in states like Montana, which is now smoke free, heart disease has dropped by as much as 60%. Now if heart disease has dropped that much this is probably a direct link to second-hand smoke. Because a state goes smoke free, everyday smokers don't stop because of the inconvenience of no smoking; but nonsmokers are simply no longer affected by its presence. Do you know anyone who is addicted to cigarette smoke even if they aren't smokers? Let me share something with you, and see if this hits home with you. Think of someone who isn't a smoker but works in a smoking-permitted atmosphere or someone who lives with a smoker but is not the one who uses tobacco. How about a waitress in a bar or restaurant that allows smoking? I have paid attention to nonsmokers who sit in a smoking section, even when they are without their partner who is the smoker.

Have you ever been to a livestock auction? I'm sure that many of you have not. I grew up going to cattle and horse auctions and spent so much time with my father there, since he brought me every week. Remember, this was in the '50s, '60s, and '70s. It was common to be next to all kinds of smokers, since we were all unaware of its negative effects. For those of you who have never been to a livestock auction, try to imagine standing shoulder to shoulder in a large barn with dirt floors, and inspecting animals up for sale. Horses or cattle were coming in and out, while being auctioned off, and the smoke was so thick in there, you could cut it with a knife. As a boy of 5 or 6 years old, when I used to attend these places with my father, I would end up going home with that smell all over me, but no one noticed back then. Imagine how much smoke my lungs consumed by just being there, if half of the 500 people there were smoking cigarettes or cigars? In today's world, you would not allow your son to stand there and breathe all that smoke in if you were a nonsmoker would you? How about this statistic then: If you are a smoker who smokes a pack a day and now 100 smokers are all around you all night long during this auction, how much smoke have you consumed? As a smoker then, you realize that if you are in a confined area, like a big barn with dirt floors smoking with other smokers, you are breathing secondhand smoke yourself? Wouldn't that be the same as smoking more than you believe to be your normal consumption, times two or three, maybe more?

I wouldn't wait for these places to go smoke free anytime soon, but as for the rest of the world, let's wait and see. In today's world, we hear so much about restaurants and office buildings becoming smoke free. My home state of Connecticut is now a smoke-free state, and Connecticut was, at one time, a very big tobacco producer. In the '30s, '40s, '50s, and '60s it was very common to see pure white cloth covering tobacco fields in northeastern Connecticut. I now live in North Carolina where tobacco is a very big product just like it used to be in Connecticut.

As Bad as Primary Smoke

Many of the largest tobacco companies were located here in North Carolina; some are still thriving. In Connecticut, there is no smoking allowed in any public places whatsoever. In

North Carolina, smoking is banned in most public buildings, malls, schools, and now all restaurants. The more we prohibit smoking in public places, the more we can count on less smoking-related health problems. Now think about this for a minute before you feel offended if you are a smoker. You might wonder how going smoke free in public is helpful to both smokers and nonsmokers alike. Even as a smoker, the less smoke you are exposed to, the better it is for you as well. In plain theory, even smokers can be affected by secondhand smoke. Do you see that? If you and a coworker smoke at the same time, you are both breathing each other's smoke besides your own. Be careful when and where you smoke.

Suppose you are driving on a long trip and your spouse is with you, and both of you smoke a pack a day. Now if secondhand smoke is all that we say it is, and you are breathing your spouse's secondhand smoke and yours as well, isn't that the same as smoking two packs a day each? Sure it is. Believe me, pre-owned smoke is as bad as primary smoke could ever be.

Do you see how breathing smoke from someone else is as bad as smoking the cigarettes yourself? Let me ask you this: Do you think secondhand smoke is addictive? A nonsmoker with enough exposure to secondhand smoke can become addicted to smoking. It most certainly is, and why wouldn't it be? We begin habits and desires from repetitiveness of foods, beverages, drugs, smoking, using profanity, and oh yes, sex as well. Now suppose you are a nonsmoker, but your father, mother, coworker, or even you work in an establishment that allows smoking. What if your spouse is a smoker and you have been so used to it that you no longer feel affected by it? So, are you still one of these who think all the hype about secondhand smoke is just that, all hype? God, I hope not, for you are wrong if you do. We are all affected by this health issue, even if you are a nonsmoker. I don't smoke anymore, but it is still an issue for me. How do you think a nonsmoker feels when walking into a restaurant or office building and sees three or four smokers standing right beside the front door smoking away? The nonsmoker still has to walk through the secondhand smoke, and that smell ends up on their clothes just the same.

Innocent Victims

One night I had to pick up a check from a guy who is a very heavy smoker. The thought of walking into his house to sit there for 10 minutes to receive a check would literally upset my stomach. And every time I had ever been in his house before, my clothes carried that smell of smoke into my car and my house as well. Hey, I don't smoke, anymore, remember? So, I politely asked if he would leave the envelope in his mailbox for me to pick up later that night. That way, I could drive by, pick it up, and not disturb him. That sounds simple enough, doesn't it? I stopped by, pulled up to the mailbox, and picked up the white envelope from the mailbox. As I started driving away, with the envelope in my SUV, I instantly smelled smoke, big time. I actually had to hold it out the window while I drove to air it out because it smelled so awful. I wish I were kidding. He has two beautiful white dogs that he would kill for, and when I asked how he felt about their breathing his secondhand smoke, he simply said they don't mind. Really? I wonder in what language they told him that. These dogs are innocent victims, and I have seen their reaction to his smoking. My uncle, Frank J. Lato, died from secondhand smoke. At age 72 and in seemingly perfect health, he was told by his doctor that he had lung cancer. He never smoked a day in his life. How then, did he get lung cancer? He was a railroad conductor on a commuter train for 40 years, collecting tickets and breathing in secondhand smoke. Here is a man who, at the age of 20-something in the 1940s, thought that working on a commuter train from New Canaan, Connecticut, to Grand Central Station, New York City, was a great job. He figured it would be a very safe bet for the future to ride a commuter train every day from Connecticut to New York. What is there to do but get up at 4 a.m., dress for work, kiss your wife Rose goodbye and head for the train? He spent 40 years doing the simplest job a man could want and never dreamed he would one day fall victim to cancer because of his work. My Uncle Tony, his brother, also worked for the railroad as a conductor, about the same time as Frank. Uncle Tony didn't put in as many hours as Uncle Frank did because he was a landscape contractor when he wasn't riding the rails, but he did the same job on the same train. Uncle Tony developed cancer and died two years after his diagnosis. He rode the same train every day, did the same job as his brother did, and ended up a cancer victim as well. Coincidence? Not likely. What about a waitress? A flight attendant or an airline passenger before the '90s when smoking was banned on flights? A bus driver? A bartender? How about any of us who have ever been out dancing at any kind of smoked-filled club? What about exposure from family members who just didn't know better?

If you are a smoker reading this [viewpoint] and you have a loved one who is the victim here, then how do you feel knowing that your secondhand smoke contributed to their health issues? Like my uncle at age 72, who was perfectly innocent going through life, he is told he has six months to live.

Addicted to Smoke

Do you think that a nonsmoker can become addicted to smoke and in fact have the same habits as a smoker? You better have said yes to this one. I know of a couple who were married for more than 45 years. The husband smoked, but the wife did not. They would eat at a local diner nearly every day. I asked them once why they sat in the smoking section when he smoked and she didn't. They would always say, "Oh, he needs his cigarettes and has to smoke." Then their daughter joined them from time to time with her children along, guess where they would sit? One day they did not come in to eat, and I found out that he had a fatal heart attack and was gone.

Take a guess where his widow sat the next time she came into the diner to eat? You probably guessed the smoking section, and you would be correct if you had. I walked over to express my condolences and asked why she was sitting in the smoking section.

I told her to come sit with us, and we would buy her breakfast.

She declined our offer. She said she wanted to sit where her husband always sat. Sentimental? With her husband gone more than five years now, she still sits in the smoking section, and now it's with a new friend who smokes. . . . She has an addiction to nicotine and the smell of smoke and has had it for years without ever realizing it herself. She is every bit the smoker her late husband was. Can you see that? Bet on this one, too, and you would be right. OK, what about her daughter? Do you think she is now becoming addicted to smoke? How about her children? They are completely innocent just like my uncle was, and what are the chances that their future will have consequences because of secondhand smoke? I like to call it used smoke because that is exactly what it is. In the car business, it would be called pre-owned smoke.

A Lesson on Influence

Laugh if you will, but it is a sad case, and it is repeated all over the world. I was in my 20s and married to that wrong woman, and on Saturday nights we would get together with two other couples to play cards. All six of us smoked. Now, for those of you who have never sat playing cards on a Saturday night, with six smokers and drinking soft drinks, here is what happens. No less than three people are smoking at any given time. Knowing what we know now, it's called awareness, all six of us are breathing smoke as long as someone is smoking. It is fair to say that all six of us smoked all night without stopping because of the secondhand smoking theory. What? Did I say "six" of us? Where are my manners? My son Frank was 10 feet above us, sleeping in his bed and breathing this used smoke. Oh, wait. Did I say seven were breathing this deadly by-product?

What about our two Great Danes? Dogs breathe air, too, don't they? It's safe to assume the Latos loved their animals just like family members. Have you ever heard of a pet dying from cancer? They sure do. Was my son innocent just like my uncle? My two dogs? Your children? Your pets? YES! One Sunday morning while I was cleaning the disgusting ashtrays from the card game the night before, my son Frank wanted to help me. He wanted to be just like his daddy, so he brought one of the dirty ashtrays (now very cold from hours ago) to the kitchen garbage can. Instead of cleaning it, he threw it away full of butts. I smiled and showed him how to clean it with a paper towel, and then put it in the sink to wash it. So he took the next ashtray, cleaned it with a paper towel and then threw it away just as before. Could be Frank was telling me something. Can you see this prime example of a bad influence here with respect to our smoking habit? My innocent little boy was finding fun in cleaning dirty ashtrays on a Sunday morning. My bad influence taught this innocent little boy about smoking by watching both his parents and then by cleaning dirty ashtrays as well. It's too bad I wasn't influenced by his idea of throwing away the ashtrays sooner. I was 28 at the time. Just think. I wasted 10 more years smoking (at a pack a day, that's 3,640 packs for those 10 years) before I threw away the ashtrays and cigarettes for good. Maybe I should have taken a lesson from my son Frank on influence. Let me ask you about the condition of our home or yours. If we were to put our house on the market after one of our late-night card games, how well do you think it would sell, if a nonsmoker looked at it? Even a smoker would notice the smell and the dingy color of the paint, drapes, furniture, etc. No matter how clean you keep your home, that smoke odor will last. The point is secondhand smoke is expensive.

How about your car? What if you go to the dealer tomorrow and ask to see how much he or she will give you on a trade? What happens if there is that smell? The ashtray is dirty.... There's a small burn in the seat, carpet, seat belts, or whatever. Do you think that will affect your trade-in price? I'll bet it does....

Awareness Counts

Let there be no bones about it, secondhand smoke is as bad as primary smoke.

It can be no better than smoking the tobacco yourself. We know about the dangers of smoking today more than ever before. Think back about people who have passed on, and no one knew why their grandfather had heart trouble, even though he didn't smoke. Could it be that he sat right beside a coworker for years who smoked? Life is so precious in many ways. Protecting yourself and loved ones can be as easy as looking both ways before you cross the street. If you continue to smoke, or if you are still trying to stop, remember the secondhand smoke theory along the way. Avoid it yourself; by all means, don't expose someone else to yours. This should include pets and children as well. Secondhand smoke is anything but second in nature. Because of its health risks, it will not come in second or even last place at your next physical. Please be very careful. Awareness counts.

> *"Statistically, the risk of secondhand smoke is far smaller than the risk of getting* lung *cancer from drinking pasteurized milk."*

The Dangers of Secondhand Smoke Are Exaggerated

Edmund Contoski

In the following viewpoint, Edmund Contoski argues that the hazards of secondhand smoke are based on ridiculous claims and lies. To promote the passage of smoking bans, he suggests, anti-smoking groups have misled the public with scientific misrepresentations and deceits about secondhand smoke. Their well-financed campaigns have overshadowed legitimate research demonstrating that secondhand smoke does not pose a statistically significant health risk, including increased risks of tobacco-related mortality and lung cancer, Contoski maintains. However, deaths attributed to smoking bans—such as smokers driving longer distances to smoke—are on the rise. Contoski is an author and retired environmental consultant.

As you read, consider the following questions:

1. According to Contoski, what ridiculous statement does the US Office of the Surgeon General make about secondhand smoke?

2. What occurred with the American Cancer Society and a major statistical study on secondhand smoke it supported, as told by Contoski?

3. What evidence does Contoski offer to back his argument that the risk of getting lung cancer from secondhand smoke is smaller than getting it from drinking pasteurized milk?

In order to get smoking bans passed, it was necessary to create an atmosphere of hatred toward the "enemy," to work people into a frenzy over a threat to their health, whether the threat was real or not. What mattered was not truth or science but whether the desired result—smoking bans—could be achieved. So truth and science were quickly sacrificed to the-end-justifies-the-means policy of antismoking organizations. Michael Siegel, MD, is both a medical doctor and public health official. He has 21 years' experience in tobacco policy research and currently teaches at the Boston University School of Public Health. Though adamantly opposed to smoking, he says: "The anti-smoking movement is driven by an agenda—an agenda that will not allow science, sound policy analysis, the law, or ethics to get in its way."

Dr. Siegel has cited over a hundred antismoking groups—including the American Cancer Society, the American Lung Association and the American Heart Association—for misleading the public with fallacious scientific claims. His website, www.tobaccoanalysis.blogspot.com, details an astonishing array of scientific misrepresentations, outright lies and hypocrisy by antismoking groups. These tactics have proven effective, even as they have become ever more shrill and absurd.

Ridiculous and Phony Claims About Secondhand Smoke

Recently Dr. Siegel ran a Most Ridiculous Secondhand Smoke Claim Tournament. The national championship was won by the St. Louis University Tobacco Prevention Center. Its winning entry introduced the scare of radioactivity from secondhand smoke by the claim that it contains plutonium-210, which does not exist anywhere in the known universe. The St. Louis group previously had claimed secondhand smoke contained asbestos. When that was debunked, it issued a correction substituting plutonium-210 for asbestos. The American Cancer Society [ACS] managed to make the Final Four in this liars tournament with this entry: "Immediate effects of secondhand smoke include cardiovascular problems such as damage to cell walls in the circulatory system, thickening of the blood and arteries, and arteriosclerosis (hardening of the arteries) or heart disease, increasing the chance of heart attack or stroke." Ridiculous though that statement is, it failed to top the entry of the St. Louis University Tobacco Prevention Center, and ACS was eliminated from the competition.

The U.S. [Office of the] Surgeon General also figured in the contest with: "Even brief exposure to secondhand smoke has immediate adverse effects on the cardiovascular system and increases risk for heart disease and lung cancer." But it went down to defeat from Action on Smoking and Health, which came up with this whopper: "Even for people without such respiratory conditions, breathing drifting tobacco smoke for even brief periods can be deadly. For example, the Centers for Disease Control [and Prevention (CDC)] has warned that breathing drifting tobacco smoke for as little as 30 minutes (less than the time one might be exposed outdoors on a beach, sitting on a park bench, listening to a concert in a park, etc.) can raise a nonsmoker's risk of suffering a fatal heart attack to that of a smoker."(!)

That such monumental lies have been instrumental in the passage of smoking bans is a measure of the gullibility and scientific illiteracy of the general public and elected officials. Of course, it is also a demonstration of the dishonesty of the smoking ban activists and the absence of genuine evidence for their cause. As the independent health consultants Littlewood & Fennel testified in their report to the National Toxicology Program's Board of Scientific Counselors, the antismoking movement is driven by "avowed anti-smoking advocates determined to somehow prove that ETS [environmental tobacco smoke] is a human carcinogen *in the face of irrefutable evidence to the contrary.*"

Studies Debunking Secondhand Smoke Are Obscured

The constant repetition of phony claims about health hazards of secondhand smoke, carried out by a well-financed campaign, has obscured the many studies debunking these claims. For example, the Congressional Research Service [CRS] concluded: "It is possible that very few or even no deaths can be attributed to ETS [environmental tobacco smoke]." Further, it stated that nonsmokers exposed to pack-a-day ETS every day for 40 years have "little or no risk of developing lung cancer"—much less dying from it. The CRS is part of the Library of Congress and has all the resources of that esteemed institution at its disposal. It is highly respected, nonpartisan, accepted by both Republicans and Democrats as fair and impartial, has no ties to tobacco companies, no regulatory or other agenda, and accepts no outside funding.

Then there was the congressional investigation by the U.S. House of Representatives of the EPA's [Environmental Protection Agency's] report on secondhand smoke. It found the EPA guilty of "conscious misuse of science and the scientific process to achieve a political agenda that could not otherwise be justified."

The American Cancer Society has sponsored at least four studies over the years, all of which failed to find any statistically significant health risk from secondhand smoke, according to the standard cited by its own director of analytic epidemiology. But that hasn't kept the ACS from claiming secondhand smoke is dangerous. The most powerful statistical study ever done on the subject was the [James] Enstrom–[Geoffrey] Kabat study. It covered 100,000 people for 38 years. The ACS financed it, helped set it up, and provided data for it until preliminary results indicated the opposite of what the ACS wanted. It then withdrew its financial support and denounced the study, which was eventually published in the *British Medical Journal*, one of the world's foremost medical journals. The study concluded: "The results do not support a causal relation between environmental tobacco smoke and tobacco-related mortality."

Statistically, the risk of secondhand smoke is far smaller than the risk of getting *lung* cancer from drinking pasteurized milk. Epidemiologists use "relative risk" (RR or risk ratio) as a means for gauging the severity of risk. The U.S. surgeon general has stated the RR for secondhand smoke is between 1.20 to 1.30. The risk for *lung* cancer from drinking pasteurized milk is 2.14. And the relative risk for getting cancer from drinking the municipal tap water that tens of millions of Americans drink every day in thousands of cities across the U.S. is 2.0 to 4.0. But where are all the dead bodies from the millions of people exposed to this far higher risk? Do you know of *any?* So how can secondhand smoke, which has a far lower relative risk, be killing thousands of people as claimed? In 2001 the International Agency for Research on Cancer, in Lyon, France, reported: "ETS exposure during childhood is not associated with an increased risk of lung cancer. No clear dose-response relationship could be demonstrated for cumulative spousal ETS exposure. . . . Even exposure to ETS from other sources was not associated with lung cancer risk."

Death by Smoking Ban

While secondhand smoke has not been shown to represent a statistically significant health risk, deaths continue to mount from smoking bans. In a recent article in the *Journal of Public*

Secondhand Smoke Is Not Closely Scrutinized

The idea that secondhand smoke is a deadly health hazard dovetails so well with the goal of discouraging smoking that tobacco opponents generally have not been inclined to scrutinize it very closely. Nevertheless, several scientists who agree that discouraging smoking is important have warned that sound science should not be compromised for that purpose. On the subject of ETS [environmental tobacco smoke], they have observed a tendency to ignore subtleties, make questionable assumptions, minimize methodological problems, and gloss over the limitations of the data. "I just think a great deal more skepticism is in order," says Geoffrey Kabat, a cancer epidemiologist who served on the advisory panel that reviewed the EPA's [Environmental Protection Agency's] report. "If these were data on something else—risk factors for ingrown toenails or something like that—people would look at it and say, 'Well, it's really not too impressive. . . . There's not that much there.'"

Jacob Sullum, For Your Own Good:
The Anti-Smoking Crusade and the Tyranny of Public Health.
New York: Simon & Schuster, 1999, p. 160.

Economics, researchers set forth evidence that smokers are driving further to where they can smoke, resulting in more fatal accidents involving alcohol. This could be due to driving longer distances to where smoking is permitted outdoors or where enforcement is unlikely, as well as driving across borders to where smoking in bars is legal. The study covered 120 counties, including 20 which banned smoking. It found that alcohol-related fatal car accidents increased 13%. For a typical county of 680,000 people, this is equivalent to about six deaths. And this pattern did not diminish over time. Where smoking bans had been in place longer than 18 months, the fatal accident rate increased 19%. The trend is especially apparent where border-hopping to smoky bars is possible—indicating very strongly the effect of smoking bans on the accident rate. Fatal accidents in Delaware County in Pennsylvania increased 26% after the adjacent state of Delaware went smoke free. And when Boulder County Colorado went smoke free, fatal accidents in adjacent Jefferson County went up by 40%.

There is also another category of deaths from smoking bans. The well-financed campaign of ever more virulent and fraudulent claims of ETS health dangers has spawned a level of hatred that has produced violence and death. We hear reports of deaths of a kind we never heard before the smoking ban campaigns. In Minneapolis, where I live, the *Star Tribune* carried an article headlined: "Man Charged with Severing Wife's Tongue and Windpipe." It states the man slashed her throat because she smoked a cigarette to celebrate her birthday. She was in critical condition, and he was charged with attempted murder. We never used to see stories like that, but here are some more:

Utah: A teenager was murdered for smoking in downtown Salt Lake City.

Ohio: Man beaten to death for not giving up cigarette. Ricardo Leon, 23, died.

UK: Nurse stabbed to death at hospital in an outside smoking area.

UK: Man killed wife and two sons over her smoking. John Jarvis, 42, stabbed his wife Patricia in the heart and then murdered their sons, John, 11, and Stuart, eight.

Louisiana: Pregnant woman shot over cigarette. 18-year-old refused to stop smoking. . . .

We didn't hear stories of these kinds of violence before the smoking ban activists started fomenting hatred with their *ji-*

had (holy war) against smoking. It's time for them to admit their lies result in killing far more people than secondhand smoke does (if it kills any at all).

Liberty Is the Only Answer

Once again, it is clear that, regardless of the good intentions of the jihadist do-gooders, lying and a policy of the end justifying the means simply do not work. Those tactics cannot make a safer world than truth, science and respect for individual rights—including property rights. Liberty is still the best answer—in fact, the only answer—to a better, safer, healthier society. But some people never learn; they keep trying to prove that force is better than freedom and individual rights. And their mistakes continue to be paid for with the blood and lives of innocent people.

Periodical and Internet Sources Bibliography

The following articles have been selected to supplement the diverse views presented in this chapter.

Emily Alpert	"Teen Cigarette Smoking Drops to Lowest Point Recorded, Study Says," *Los Angeles Times*, July 12, 2013.
Melissa Dahl	"Too Many American Teens Are Smoking 'Little Cigars,' Report Says," NBC News, October 22, 2013.
Brady Dennis	"Surgeon General Report Links More Diseases, Health Problems to Smoking Tobacco," *Washington Post*, January 17, 2014.
Economist	"The Cigarette Industry: Running Out of Puff," January 25, 2014.
Sophie Egan	"Why Smoking Rates Are at New Lows," *New York Times*, June 25, 2013.
Daniel Fisher	"Study Finds No Link Between Secondhand Smoke and Cancer," *Forbes*, December 12, 2013.
Nirvi Shah	"Teenagers and Tobacco," *Education Week*, December 12, 2012.
Alexandra Sifferlin	"The Major Toll of Secondhand Smoke," *Time*, September 21, 2012.
Rob Stein	"Wanna Smoke? It Could Cost You a Tooth, FDA Warns Teens," NPR, February 4, 2014.
Lauren Tarshis	"Teens vs. Cigarettes: Are Tobacco Companies Targeting Teens?," *Choices*, April 2013.
Ali Walton	"Why Teen Smoking's on the Rise," *Salon*, November 9, 2013.

OPPOSING
VIEWPOINTS®
SERIES

CHAPTER 2

How Can Tobacco Use Be Reduced?

Chapter Preface

The nicotine patch is a type of nicotine replacement therapy (NRT) to aid in smoking cessation. Obtainable in the United States without a prescription since 1996, the patch resembles an adhesive bandage and delivers nicotine transdermally, meaning through the skin. It is available in various strengths and sizes; users progress to patches with lower dosages every few weeks to ease out of nicotine addiction. Depending on their smoking habits and withdrawal symptoms, some people wear a sixteen-hour patch and others wear a twenty-four-hour patch. It is approved by the US Food and Drug Administration for use up to five months.

Although users are instructed not to smoke while wearing the patch, researchers at Duke University's medical center claim that concurrent use safely doubles successful cessation rates. In a July 2009 article at the ScienceDaily website, Jed Rose, who directs the Duke Center for Smoking Cessation, said that "people who use the patch before quitting are likely to spontaneously reduce the number of cigarettes they smoke because the patch satisfies their need for nicotine and makes the act of smoking less enjoyable." Rose adds that monitoring the user's smoking habits before quitting can help determine if the patch is working. "If the smoker is not spontaneously decreasing the number of cigarettes they are smoking, we may be able to find a different treatment that will work for them rather than letting them stay on an ineffective treatment and fail," he proposes.

Nonetheless, a study by researchers at the Harvard School of Public Health and the University of Massachusetts Boston suggests that NRT, including patches, are ineffective overall in aiding smoking cessation. Surveying participants from 2001 to 2006, researchers reported no difference in relapse rates among those using them for at least six weeks—with or without counseling—and no difference in successful cessation rates among heavy or light smokers using NRT. "This study shows that using NRT is no more effective in helping people stop smoking cigarettes in the long-term than trying to quit on one's own," maintains Hillel Alpert, lead author of the study and research scientist at the Harvard School of Public Health. In the following chapter, the authors deliberate the measures sought to reduce smoking and tobacco use.

> *"The tobacco industry and its allies continually oppose tobacco tax increases because they know that price increases will reduce the number of 'replacement smokers' that they need to sustain their business as well as encourage current smokers to quit."*

Increasing Tobacco Taxes Would Reduce Tobacco Use

Campaign for Tobacco-Free Kids

The Campaign for Tobacco-Free Kids is a nonprofit organization advocating public policies that prevent youth smoking, promote smoking cessation, and reduce secondhand smoke. In the following viewpoint, it asserts that increasing tobacco taxes reduces tobacco use across a range of groups, from youths to pregnant women. Trends show that rising cigarette prices are strongly correlated with declining consumption, maintains the campaign, and evidence from states' experiences reveals that tobacco tax increases translate into greater numbers of smokers seeking assistance to quit. Aware of the impacts, tobacco companies employ numerous strategies to reduce the costs of their products, the campaign alleges.

As you read, consider the following questions:

1. How would a tax increasing cigarette prices by 10 percent impact smoking among pregnant women, as proposed by the author?

2. According to the viewpoint, how did the 2009 federal tobacco tax increase affect students who smoke?

3. What strategies do tobacco companies use to reduce the prices of their products, as described by the author?

[It] is clear that price has a pronounced effect on the smoking prevalence of teenagers, and that the goals of reducing teenage smoking and balancing the budget would both be served by increasing the federal excise tax on cigarettes.

—Philip Morris research
executive Myron Johnston

Peer-reviewed economic studies and past experiences show beyond a doubt that tobacco tax increases reduce tobacco use, especially among youth. In fact, data show that the most recent federal tobacco tax increase (on April 1, 2009) effectively reduced youth tobacco use rates. The tobacco industry and its allies continually oppose tobacco tax increases because they know that price increases will reduce the number of "replacement smokers" that they need to sustain their business as well as encourage current smokers to quit.

Economic Research Confirms That Tobacco Tax Increases Reduce Tobacco Use

Numerous economic studies in peer-reviewed journals have documented the impact of cigarette tax increases and other price hikes on both adult and underage smoking. The general consensus from these studies is that every ten percent increase in the real price of cigarettes will reduce the prevalence of adult smoking by approximately three to five percent and reduce teen smoking by about seven percent. This research indicates that raising the federal cigarette tax rate to produce a ten percent increase in cigarette prices would reduce the number of current youth smokers by more than 350,000. Research studies have also found that:

- Cigarette price and tax increases work even more effectively to reduce smoking among males, blacks, Hispanics, and lower-income smokers.

- A cigarette tax increase that raises prices by ten percent will reduce smoking among pregnant women by seven percent, preventing thousands of miscarriages and stillborn births, and saving tens of thousands of newborns from suffering from smoking-affected births and related health consequences.

- Higher taxes on smokeless tobacco reduce its use, particularly among young males; and increasing cigar prices through tax increases reduces adult and youth cigar smoking.

- By reducing smoking levels, cigarette tax increases reduce secondhand smoke exposure among nonsmokers, especially children.

Increasing U.S. Cigarette Prices and Declining Consumption

Comparing the trends in cigarette prices and overall U.S. cigarette consumption from 1970 to 2011 shows a strong correlation between increasing prices and decreasing consumption. As a result of the 2009 federal tax increase, cigarette pack sales declined by a record 8.3 percent in 2009—the largest decline since 1932.

U.S. cigarette prices are largely controlled by the cigarette companies' price-setting decisions. But from 2000 to 2011, the federal tax on cigarettes also increased from 34 cents to $1.01 per pack (and the average state cigarette tax increased from 42 cents to $1.46 per pack). Without these tax increases, U.S. smoking levels would certainly be much higher. . . .

Prices and Youth Smoking Rates

Youth smoking prevalence is tied to cigarette pack prices. As prices climbed in the late 1990s and early 2000s, youth smoking rates declined sharply, but as the price decreased between 2003 and 2005 (along with funding for tobacco prevention programs in many states), youth rates increased. After the most recent 61.66 cent federal cigarette tax rate increase on April 1, 2009, youth rates declined, as expected.

Further, researchers looked more closely at the effect of the 2009 federal tobacco tax increase and found a substantial and immediate impact on youth smoking and smokeless tobacco use. The percentage of students who reported smoking in the past 30 days dropped between 9.7 percent and 13.3 percent immediately following the tax increase, resulting in an estimated 220,000 to 287,000 fewer current smokers among middle and high school students in May 2009. Similarly, youth smokeless tobacco use declined between 16 to 24 percent immediately after the rate increase, resulting in an estimated 135,000 to 203,000 fewer youth smokeless tobacco users in the same period.

State Experiences with Cigarette Tax Increases Show They Encourage Quit Attempts and Reduce Smoking

Evidence shows that cigarette tax increases are prompting many smokers to quit—directly translating into lower future smoking rates. For example, when the 2009 federal tobacco tax increase went into effect, state quit lines received record numbers of calls from people who wanted assistance in quitting tobacco use. The Wisconsin quit line received a record-breaking 20,000 calls in the first two months after its $1.00 per cigarette pack increase (it typically receives 9,000 calls per

Taxing Tobacco Reduces the Instant Gratification of Smoking

Decisions about smoking are similar to those about retirement saving. People want to save, but it is hard because spending provides instant gratification; mechanisms such as automatic deductions from people's paychecks can help people avoid the spending temptation. Similarly, the tobacco tax reduces the instant gratification of smoking and leads some smokers to put more weight on its long-term risks.

Chuck Marr and Chye-Ching Huang,
"Higher Tobacco Taxes Can Improve Health and Raise Revenue,"
Center on Budget and Policy Priorities, March 19, 2014.

year). And in Washington State, adult smoking declined from 22.6 to 19.7 percent in the year after its 60 cent cigarette tax increase in 2002, reducing the number of adult smokers in the state by more than 100,000. In fact, Michigan's state quit line had to temporarily shut down because it ran out of funds after offering free nicotine replacement therapy to callers who were quitting in preparation for the federal tobacco tax increase. These are but a few of dozens of examples of declines in smoking following state tobacco tax increases. Indeed, the ten states with the lowest smoking rates have an average state tobacco tax of $2.32, compared to an average tax of 72 cents in the ten states with the highest smoking rates.

Expert Conclusions: Tobacco Tax Increases Reduce Use

- The 2012 surgeon general's report, "Preventing Tobacco Use Among Youth and Young Adults," concluded that "most of the research over the past decade has concluded that increases in cigarette prices lead to reductions in the prevalence of smoking and its intensity among youth and young adults." The report further stated, "Tobacco control policies, including higher taxes on smokeless tobacco . . . are effective in reducing the use of smokeless tobacco among adolescent males. . . ."

- In December 2008, the Goldman Sachs tobacco industry outlook for 2009 concluded that a 61 cent federal cigarette tax rate increase would reduce cigarette consumption in the USA by seven percent. Other Wall Street tobacco industry analysts have also recently concluded that an increase to the federal cigarette tax would significantly reduce smoking levels.

- In its 2007 report, "Ending the Tobacco Problem: A Blueprint for the Nation," the National Academy of Sciences' Institute of Medicine recommends raising cigarette taxes in states with low rates and the federal cigarette excise tax and indexing them to inflation, to reduce cigarette consumption and to provide money for tobacco control. The report states, "an increase in the federal excise tax would have the dual purposes of reducing consumption and making more funds available for tobacco control programs," thus "the committee thinks that the federal tobacco excise tax rate should be increased substantially—at least on the order of $1.00 per pack . . .".

- The President's Cancer Panel's 2007 report, "Promoting Healthy Lifestyles," advised an increase in the federal tobacco tax, stating, "Increasing this tax would not only contribute to reducing smoking initiation and prevalence, but potentially would be an important source of revenue for federally-funded tobacco use prevention and control efforts."

- The 2003 "A National Action Plan for Tobacco Cessation" from the Interagency Committee on Smoking and Health, appointed by the Department of Health and Human Service secretary Tommy Thompson, recommended, "the [federal] excise tax increase has the following virtues: (1) of all the recommended components of the National Action Plan for Tobacco Cessation, research suggests that the excise tax increase would have the largest immediate impact on tobacco use; (2) it would pay for all other plan elements [to help smokers quit]; and (3) it would satisfy the need expressed repeatedly in public testimony for a stable, dedicated funding source for tobacco cessation initiatives."

- The 2000 U.S. surgeon general's report, "Reducing Tobacco Use," found that raising tobacco-product prices decreases the prevalence of tobacco use, particularly among kids and young adults, and that tobacco tax increases produce "substantial long-term improvements in health." From its review of existing research, the report concluded that raising tobacco taxes is one of the most effective tobacco prevention and control strategies.

- In its 1998 report, "Taking Action to Reduce Tobacco Use," the National Academy of Sciences' Institute of Medicine concluded that "the single most direct and reliable method for reducing consumption is to increase the price of tobacco products, thus encouraging the cessation and reducing the level of initiation of tobacco use."

Tobacco Companies Know Tobacco Tax Increases Reduce Tobacco Use

Tobacco companies have opposed tobacco tax increases by arguing that raising prices does not reduce smoking. But the companies' internal documents that were disclosed in the tobacco lawsuits and financial filings with the U.S. Securities and Exchange Commission show that they have known for decades that raising cigarette taxes is one of the most effective ways to prevent and reduce smoking, especially among kids. For instance, the quote at the beginning of this [viewpoint] demonstrates that knowledge. This is, of course, why they strongly oppose tobacco tax increases. For example, in 2012, the big tobacco companies spent more than $45 million to defeat a tobacco tax increase initiative in California and have spent similar amounts or more (per capita) in other states.

Since the companies know that price increases will reduce use, they use a variety of strategies to reduce product prices, including multipack offers (i.e., buy one, get one free), buy downs (where the company contracts with retailers to offer lower prices on products), and coupons—all to encourage tobacco users to continue using and make the products more affordable to youth. Those efforts seem to be effective; the 2012 surgeon general's report stated, "it can be concluded that the industry's extensive use of price-reducing promotions has led to higher rates of tobacco use among young people than would have occurred in the absence of these promotions."

Maximizing the Public Health Benefits (and New Revenues) from Tobacco Tax Rate Increases

When the federal excise tax rate on cigarettes is increased, raising the federal tax rates on all other tobacco products to a parallel level will prevent smokers from simply switching to other lower-taxed tobacco products and thus reducing the health and revenue benefits of the tax. This kind of switching has been quite pronounced lately—largely because of much lower federal and state tax rates on cigars, pipe tobacco, and smokeless tobacco. Tobacco companies have even manipulated their products by changing the wrapper, increasing the weight, and changing the labels to meet definitions of other tobacco products in order to evade taxes. As a result of these evasion strategies, sales of large cigars increased, while sales of small cigars decreased, even though the cigars sold remained largely the same. Similarly, sales of products labeled as "pipe tobacco," which was really just roll-your-own [RYO] tobacco in re-named bags increased dramatically while sales in the RYO category declined. The U.S. Government Accountability Office (GAO) found that the higher tax rates on cigarettes and small cigars compared to large cigars "created an incentive for producers to modify products to qualify as large cigars according to TTB [U.S. Alcohol and Tobacco Tax and Trade Bureau]."

In addition, small tax rate increases (less than about 10 percent of the average pack price) do not usually produce significant public health benefits or cost savings because cigarette companies can easily offset the beneficial impact of such small rate increases with temporary price cuts, coupons, and other promotional discounting. Likewise, splitting a tax rate increase into separate, smaller increases in successive years will sharply diminish or eliminate the public health benefits and related cost savings (as well as reduce the total amount of new revenues).

> *"Tobacco tax hikes entail serious fiscal consequences for smokers and non-smokers alike."*

Increasing Tobacco Taxes Would Have Unintended Consequences

Diana Oprinescu

In the following viewpoint, Diana Oprinescu proposes five major reasons why tobacco tax increases have unintended consequences for taxpayers, not just smokers. First, she contends that states with low tobacco taxes have lower tax burdens, indicating that tobacco tax hikes are associated with higher taxation overall. Then, Oprinescu says that tobacco taxes almost never reduce other taxes and do not enable general tax cuts. These tax hikes also do not delay tax increases, she adds. Oprinescu further maintains that tobacco tax increases encourage other tax hikes; revenues typically fall short of states' projections, leading states to seek additional taxpayer money. Finally, she purports that these taxes do not spur economic growth. Based in Milwaukee, Wisconsin, the author is a research assistant at Marquette University.

Diana Oprinescu, "Tobacco Taxes: Problems, Not Solutions, for Taxpayers and Budgets," *NTUF Issue Brief* online, July 31, 2013. www.ntu.org. Copyright © 2013 National Taxpayers Union. All rights reserved. Reproduced with permission.

As you read, consider the following questions:

1. What evidence does Oprinescu offer to support her position that tobacco taxes do not delay other tax increases?

2. In Oprinescu's view, how are consumers a reason tobacco tax revenues are missed?

3. What is the author's opinion of tobacco taxes and the growth of government?

After the politicking and debate associated with their passage has died down, what are the actual consequences of cigarette and other tobacco tax increases? The following National Taxpayers Union Foundation (NTUF) study examines the budgetary impact of these policies.

Proponents of cigarette tax increases often claim that only a "sinful" minority, smokers, will be affected by them. However, tobacco tax hikes entail serious fiscal consequences for smokers and nonsmokers alike, for five major reasons:

1. States with low cigarette taxes have lower overall tax burdens.

2. Tobacco tax hikes are rarely used to cut other taxes.

3. Tobacco taxes don't forestall other tax increases.

4. Tobacco tax hikes may encourage other tax hikes down the road.

5. Cigarette taxes don't spur economic growth.

This [viewpoint] demonstrates these conclusions to be valid regardless of a fluctuating economy (expansion, recession, recovery), and brings additional evidence to support the hypothesis that cigarette taxes represent an unreliable source of revenue.

1. States with Low Cigarette Taxes Have Lower Overall Tax Burdens

The most recent statistical data available shows that states with the highest cigarette taxes in the nation often have remarkably higher-than-average tax burdens; conversely, in states where cigarette taxes are lowest, total tax loads are almost always below the national average.

More specifically, in the 16 places where the per-pack cigarette tax was highest, the average per capita state and local tax burden was $1,356 above the national average. This means that the tax pressure on residents of high cigarette tax states was 39.4 percent heavier than the U.S. average in fiscal year 2010.

On the other hand, when analyzing the 15 states with the lowest per-pack cigarette tax in the nation, the total tax burden was $892 below the national average (or 21.6 percent less).

These results strongly support the hypothesis that cigarette tax hikes are associated with the political tendency of raising taxes on other activities and products, which affect smokers and nonsmokers alike.

2. Tobacco Tax Hikes Are Rarely Used to Cut Other Taxes

One argument sometimes made in favor of tobacco tax hikes holds that such an increase encourages general tax cuts; however, such arguments are disproved by statistical evidence.

It can be possible for some tobacco tax hikes to be compensated by cuts in other taxes—for instance, in fiscal year 2010, a revenue action that increased the tobacco tax in Texas was offset by other tax decreases, leading to a net reduction of $18 million. It is much more common, however, for tobacco tax hikes to be followed either by other tax increases, or by tax cuts that are worth less than the tobacco tax increase.

Thus, between 2008 and 2013, only two out of 40 revenue actions that raised the tobacco tax were followed by cuts in other taxes. Furthermore, if the results presented in a 2008 National Taxpayers Union (NTU) study are also accounted for, it can be seen that only four of 103 tobacco tax increases between 2001 and 2013 (less than 4 percent) were offset by other tax cuts. The conclusion that states imposing tobacco tax hikes don't refund the revenue elsewhere, but spend it instead, is therefore strongly reinforced.

3. Tobacco Taxes Don't Forestall Other Tax Increases

Not only are tobacco tax hikes not offset by cuts in other taxes, but they also tend to be followed by revenue actions that raise taxes on other products and services within a short period of time. . . .

Between fiscal years 2007 and 2011, 25 of 37 tobacco tax increases were followed by additional tax hikes. If the findings of the previous NTU study are also considered in the tally, a total of 66 out of 96 tobacco tax increases between fiscal years 2001 and 2011 were followed by other tax hikes during the next two years. This means that, in almost 70 percent of cases, tobacco tax hikes also affected nonsmokers because other tax increases followed.

4. Tobacco Tax Hikes May Encourage Other Tax Hikes Down the Road

Why are tobacco tax hikes likely to encourage other tax increases in the long run? To begin with, politicians often justify such actions by saying that they can use the additional revenue to plug budget deficits and/or fund programs in areas like health care or education.

Furthermore, states often fail to provide accurate estimates of how much money they will collect from cigarette tax hikes. As revenues usually fall short of these projections, additional

Revenue Estimates from Tobacco Tax Hikes as Compared to Actual Tobacco Tax Revenues

Calendar Year When the Tax Increase Took Effect	Number of States with Cigarette/ Tobacco Tax Hikes*	Number of States Where Revenue Projections Were Met
2011	5	1
2010	5	2
2009	14	4
2008	8	2
2007	9	2
2006	6	0
2005	11	6
2004	7	2
2003	15	6
2002	19	3
2001	2	1

*Data for a small number of states that increased the cigarette/tobacco tax could not be found, but the impact on the overall result could only be negligible.

Source: Compiled from budget documents, bills, and statistical data provided by the Department of Revenue in each state, and FTA data.

TAKEN FROM: Diana Oprinescu, "Tobacco Taxes: Problems, Not Solutions, for Taxpayers and Budgets," National Taxpayers Union, July 31, 2013.

taxpayer money is sought in order to continue to fund the programs and avoid budget cuts. . . .

Initial revenue projections were met in only 29 of 101 cases where cigarette/tobacco taxes were increased between 2001 and 2011. This means there is a 70 percent chance that a revenue estimate will be missed. Moreover, as only 18 of 60 revenue projections were met between 2001 and 2006 (again, a 70 percent chance of failure), these estimates remain equally unreliable in an "up," as well as in a "down," economy.

There are several possible reasons why revenue estimates are usually missed. Even while elected officials make promises about a golden pot of revenues, the percentage of adults who smoke has been declining. The latter fact alone makes accurate forecasts difficult, especially on a state or local basis. Thus, there is an inevitable tension between supporters' claims that tax hikes will both lead to bigger treasuries for governments and encourage less smoking. Indeed, political leaders may have the incentive to exaggerate revenue outcomes in order to initially enlist more constituents in favor of the tax.

Second, consumers often supplant cigarettes with alternative products that are taxed at lower rates. For instance, after a 2013 cigarette tax hike, store owners in Minnesota began to stock smoking alternatives such as e-cigarettes or "roll-your-own," for which demand was on the rise. At the federal level, the 2009 cigarette tax hike led to market shifts from roll-your-own to pipe tobacco and from small to large cigarettes, with federal revenue losses estimated to range from $615 million to $1.1 billion. Third, high taxes encourage either cross-border shopping, leading smokers to make their purchases in neighboring states with lower taxes, or smuggling. For example, media reports show that many New Yorkers used to ride the ferry to neighboring Vermont in 2010, where they paid only $22.40 instead of $43.50 . . . for one carton of cigarettes. As for smuggling, a study by the Mackinac Center for Public Policy in Michigan estimated that New York was the highest net importer of smuggled cigarettes in 2011, which accounted for 60.9 percent of the total market.

The anti-tobacco lobby usually responds to such arguments by saying that cigarette tax hikes *always* lead to at least some increased revenue for states, even if actual collections sometimes fail to meet the initial targets. However, this is not *always* the case—probably the most notorious counterexample is New Jersey, where cigarette tax revenues *dropped* by $52 million right after a tax hike in 2006.

5. Cigarette Taxes Don't Spur Economic Growth

Finally, the argument that cigarette taxes foster economic growth by bringing additional revenue to the state budget is also contradicted by recent data.

Thus, on average, the state-level governments that enacted tobacco tax increases in 2009 had a lower growth rate (1.09 percent less) than those that didn't implement such increases. This casts serious doubt on the pro-tax argument, according to which governments are able to spur growth by boosting taxes.

The foregoing research provides considerable evidence that tobacco tax hikes tend to increase the overall tax burden, are rarely associated with general tax cuts, and, rather, are frequently followed by other tax increases. Also, they do not facilitate economic growth.

Furthermore, tobacco taxes encourage the growth of government regardless of whether the business cycle is in its expansionary or in its recessionary phase. The analysis presented in this [viewpoint] supports the hypothesis that revenues obtained from tobacco tax hikes are unpredictable, because estimates are rarely met. Ultimately it can be concluded that tobacco taxes affect nonsmokers as well and that taxpayers bear high costs when the size of government expands on the basis of such an inconsistent revenue stream.

> "100% smoke-free environments are the only proven way to adequately protect the health of people from the harmful effects of secondhand tobacco smoke because no level of exposure is acceptable."

Protect People from Tobacco Smoke

World Health Organization

The World Health Organization (WHO) is the directing and coordinating authority for health within the United Nations system. In the following viewpoint, WHO claims that smoking bans are the only effective way of protecting people from secondhand smoke. These policies reduce such exposure between 80 to 90 percent in high-exposure settings, the organization points out, and workers in smoke-free workplaces are exposed to three to eight times less secondhand smoke than other workers. WHO continues that there is no safe level of exposure, making ventilation and designated smoking areas ineffective. The health impacts of smoking bans are immediate, with bar workers and general populations quickly experiencing reductions in tobacco-related symptoms and conditions, states the organization.

As you read, consider the following questions:

1. Why must governments maintain strong support of smoke-free laws, as recommended by WHO?

2. As stated by WHO, why are designated smoking areas ineffective at reducing exposure to secondhand smoke?

3. How do smoke-free environments benefit smokers, according to the organization?

The International Agency for Research on Cancer concluded: "there is sufficient evidence that implementation of smoke-free policies substantially decreases second-hand smoke exposure" (46). Studies of the effects of smoke-free policies consistently show that these policies decrease exposure to secondhand tobacco smoke by 80–90% in high-exposure settings, and that they can lead to overall decreases in exposure of up to 40% (47). People who work in places that are smoke-free are exposed to 3–8 times less secondhand tobacco smoke than other workers (48). Nonsmoking adults who live in communities with comprehensive smoke-free laws are 5–10 times less likely to be exposed to secondhand tobacco smoke than those who live where there is no smoke-free legislation (49). Ireland provides strong evidence of the effects of reducing exposure to secondhand tobacco smoke. Following the country's implementation of smoke-free legislation in 2004, ambient air nicotine and particulate matter concentrations in monitored indoor environments decreased by 83%, and there was a 79% reduction in exhaled breath carbon monoxide and an 81% reduction in salivary cotinine among bar workers. Bar workers' exposure to secondhand tobacco smoke plunged from 30 hours per week to zero (50, 51).

These findings were confirmed in numerous other places that enacted comprehensive smoke-free legislation. In Toronto, Canada, a complete smoke-free law for bars implemented in 2004 led to a reduction of 68% in the level of urinary cotinine* of bar workers in one month, while bar workers of a control community without smoke-free legislation did not experience any significant change in the level of urinary cotinine levels (52). In Scotland, comprehensive smoke-free legislation enacted in 2006 resulted in an 86% decrease in the concentration of airborne particulate matter in pubs (53) and a 39% reduction in salivary cotinine levels among adult nonsmokers (47).

In New York State, salivary cotinine levels in nonsmoking adults decreased 47% in the year after enactment of a comprehensive smoking ban in 2003 (54); in New Zealand, comprehensive smoke-free legislation enacted in 2004 appears to have reduced exposure of bar patrons to secondhand tobacco smoke by about 90% (55); and in Finland, a nationally implemented smoke-free law resulted in a reduction in secondhand tobacco smoke exposure in workplaces covered by this law, from 51% of workers reporting exposure before the law to 12% reporting exposure three years after the law became effective (56).

Enforcement Needed to Ensure Protection Against Secondhand Tobacco Smoke

Based on the scientific evidence, the Conference of the Parties to the WHO [World Health Organization] Framework Convention of Tobacco Control (WHO FCTC) has concluded that 100% smoke-free environments are the only proven way to adequately protect the health of people from the harmful effects of secondhand tobacco smoke because no level of exposure is acceptable.

Once smoke-free laws have been enacted, governments must maintain strong support through active and uniform enforcement that achieves high compliance levels, at least until

---

* Analysis of salivary or urinary cotinine concentrations is used as a biological marker to measure exposure to secondhand tobacco smoke.

such time as the law becomes self-enforcing. Although an increasing number of countries have passed legislation mandating smoke-free environments, the overwhelming majority of countries have no smoke-free laws, very limited laws, or ineffective enforcement. Legislation that is comprehensive, but that is not well enforced, does not protect against secondhand tobacco smoke exposure, and legislation that covers only some places, even if well enforced, also does not provide significant protection.

Full enforcement of smoke-free laws is critical to establishing their credibility, especially immediately following their enactment (57). It may be necessary to actively and publicly enforce the law in the period directly after smoke-free laws are enacted to demonstrate the government's commitment to ensuring compliance. Unannounced inspections by the appropriate government agency can be very effective.

Once a high level of compliance is achieved, it may be feasible to reduce the level of formal enforcement, as maintenance of smoke-free places is largely self-enforcing in areas where the public and business communities support smoke-free policies and legislation. Placing the responsibility for enforcing smoke-free places on facility owners and managers is the most effective way to ensure that the laws are enforced. In many countries, laws have established that business owners have a legal duty to provide safe workplaces for their employees. Levying of fines and other sanctions against business owners is more likely to ensure compliance than fining individual smokers.

Enforcement of legislation and its impact should be regularly monitored. Assessing and publicizing the lack of negative impact on business following enactment of smoke-free legislation will further enhance compliance with and acceptance of smoke-free laws.

Ventilation and Designated Smoking Rooms Are Not Effective

Smoking anywhere in a building significantly increases concentrations of secondhand tobacco smoke, even in parts of the building where people do not smoke (58). Physically separating smokers from nonsmokers by allowing smoking only in designated smoking rooms reduces exposure to secondhand tobacco smoke only by about half, and thus provides only partial protection (59).

The American Society of Heating, Refrigerating and Air-Conditioning Engineers concluded in 2005 that comprehensive smoke-free laws are the only effective means of eliminating the risks associated with secondhand tobacco smoke, and that ventilation techniques should not be relied upon to control health risks from secondhand tobacco smoke exposure (60, 61). This position statement concurs with other findings that ventilation and designated smoking rooms do not prevent exposure to secondhand tobacco smoke (62, 63).

Health Impact of Smoke-Free Regulations

Smoke-free laws reduce respiratory symptoms.

Because of the immediate drop in pollution levels and secondhand tobacco smoke exposure after implementation of smoke-free laws (64), improvements in respiratory health are experienced very quickly. In Scotland, bar workers reported a 26% decrease in respiratory symptoms, and asthmatic bar workers had reduced airway inflammation within three months after comprehensive, smoke-free legislation was enacted (65). In California, bartenders reported a 59% reduction in respiratory symptoms and a 78% reduction in sensory irritation symptoms within eight weeks after implementation of the law requiring bars to be smoke free (66).

Smoke-free laws reduce illness from heart disease.

Even low-level exposure to secondhand tobacco smoke has a clinically significant effect on cardiovascular disease risk

(67). Smoke-free environments reduce the incidence of heart attack among the general population almost immediately, even in the first few months after being implemented (68). Several studies have confirmed decreases in hospital admissions for heart attacks after comprehensive smoke-free legislation was enacted (69–74). Moreover, many of these studies, conducted in subnational areas (states/provinces and cities) where smoke-free laws had not been enacted on a national level, show not only the impact of such laws, but also the potential benefit of enacting smoke-free legislation on a local level when national bans are not in place.

Smoke-free laws are expected to reduce lung cancer.

Because of the long time lag between secondhand smoke exposure and the development of lung cancer, complete data are not yet available regarding the expected decline in lung cancer after implementation of smoke-free policies. Between 1988 and 2004, a period during which the state of California implemented comprehensive smoke-free legislation, rates of lung and bronchial cancer declined four times faster in California than in the rest of the United States, although at least some of this decrease may result from the sharper decline in smoking prevalence experienced in California compared with the rest of the country that began in the early 1980s (75).

Other Benefits of Smoke-Free Regulations

Smoke-free laws help smokers to reduce smoking or quit.

Smoke-free environments not only protect nonsmokers, they reduce tobacco use in continuing smokers by 2–4 cigarettes a day (76) and help smokers who want to quit, as well as former smokers who have already stopped, to quit successfully over the long term. Per capita cigarette consumption in the United States is between 5% and 20% lower in states with comprehensive smoke-free laws than in states without such laws (77).

Complete workplace smoking bans implemented in several industrialized nations are estimated to have reduced smoking prevalence among workers by an average of 3.8%, reduced average tobacco consumption by 3.1 cigarettes per day among workers who continue to smoke, and reduced total tobacco consumption among workers by an average of 29% (78). People who work in environments with smoke-free policies are nearly twice as likely to quit smoking as those in work sites without such policies, and people who continue to smoke decrease their average daily consumption by nearly four cigarettes per day (79).

After comprehensive smoke-free legislation was enacted in Ireland, about 46% of smokers reported that the law had made them more likely to quit; among those who did quit, 80% reported that the law had helped them to quit and 88% reported that the law helped them to maintain cessation (80). In Scotland, 44% of people who quit smoking said that smoke-free legislation had helped them to quit (81).

Smoke-free laws encourage establishment of smoke-free homes.

Legislation mandating smoke-free public places also encourages families to make their homes smoke free (82), which protects children and other family members from exposure to secondhand tobacco smoke (83). In Australia, the introduction of smoke-free workplace laws in the 1990s was accompanied by a steep increase in the proportion of adults who avoided exposing children to secondhand tobacco smoke in the home (84). Even smokers are likely to voluntarily implement a "no smoking" rule in their homes after comprehensive smoke-free legislation is enacted (85, 86).

Voluntary smoke-free home policies also decrease adult and youth smoking. Home smoking bans reduce progression to smoking experimentation among youths who live with nonsmokers. Teenagers who live in homes where smoking is allowed are nearly twice as likely to start smoking, even if adults are nonsmokers themselves, than in homes where smoking is prohibited (87).

Smoke-Free Laws Are Popular

Public opinion surveys show that smoke-free legislation is extremely popular wherever it is enacted, even among smokers, and that support tends to increase over time after these laws are in place. Support is generally strongest for making hospitals and other health-care facilities smoke free, while there is usually the least support for making bars and pubs smoke free (88–90).

In 2006, Uruguay became the first country in the Americas to become 100% smoke free by enacting a ban on smoking in all public spaces and workplaces, including bars, restaurants and casinos. The law won support from eight out of every 10 Uruguayans, including nearly two-thirds of the country's smokers (91). After New Zealand passed smoke-free laws in 2004, 69% of its citizens said they supported the right of people to work in a smoke-free environment (92).

The smoke-free workplace law introduced in Ireland in March 2004 has been judged successful by 96% of people, including 89% of smokers (93). In California, 75% of the population approved of smoke-free workplace laws that included restaurants and bars within the first few years after being enacted by that state in 1998 (94).

Although China has few smoke-free public places, 90% of people living in large cities—smokers and nonsmokers alike—support a ban on smoking on public transport and in schools and hospitals (95). More than 80% of urban residents in China support smoke-free legislation in workplaces, and about half support banning smoking in restaurants and bars. Russia, which also has few restrictions on smoking in public places, nearly a third of people support a complete ban on smoking in restaurants (96).

Smoke-Free Laws Do Not Hurt Business

Despite tobacco and hospitality industry claims, experience shows that in every country where comprehensive smoke-free legislation has been enacted, smoke-free environments are popular, easy to implement and enforce, and result in either a neutral or positive impact on businesses, including the hospitality sector (97, 98). These findings were similar in all places studied, including in Australia, Canada, the United Kingdom and the United States (99); Norway (100); New Zealand (101); the state of California (102); New York City (103); and various US states and municipalities (104).

In New York City, which implemented smoke-free legislation in two stages (covering most workplaces including most restaurants in 1995 and adding bars and remaining restaurants in 2003), restaurant employment increased after enactment of the 1995 law (105). Combined bar and restaurant employment and receipts increased in the year after enactment of the 2003 ordinance (103), and have continued increasing since.

After comprehensive smoke-free legislation was implemented, there were no statistically significant changes observed among hospitality industry economic indicators in Massachusetts (106), no economic harm to bar and restaurant businesses reported in the mid-sized US city of Lexington, Kentucky (107), and no adverse economic impact on tourism in Florida (108). When bars located in communities with smoke-free laws were sold, they commanded prices comparable to prices paid for similar bars in areas with no restrictions on smoking (109). This type of economic evidence can be used to counter false tobacco industry claims that establishing smoke-free places causes economic harm (97, 110).

Tobacco Industry Efforts to Avoid 100% Smoke-Free Legislation

The tobacco industry has long known that sidestream secondhand tobacco smoke contains higher concentrations of carcinogenic substances than does mainstream tobacco smoke (7). In a confidential 1978 report, the industry described increasing public concerns about secondhand tobacco smoke exposure as "the most dangerous development to the viability of the tobacco industry that has yet occurred" (111). The industry acknowledges the effectiveness of smoke-free environments, and how creating exceptions can undermine their impact. A 1992 internal report by Philip Morris stated: "Total prohibition of smoking in the workplace strongly affects industry volume. . . . Milder workplace restrictions, such as smoking only in designated areas, have much less impact on quitting rates and very little effect on consumption" (112).

The tobacco industry has a history of creating the appearance of scientific controversy in an attempt to counter initiatives intended to restrict tobacco use. However, the ultimate goal of these types of industry-backed initiatives is to maintain the social acceptability of smoking and prevent adoption of meaningful smoke-free policies in public places and in workplaces (113). Measures such as ventilation and separate smoking rooms, promoted as "reasonable" accommodations by the tobacco industry, also undermine the intended effects of legislative measures by continuing to expose people to secondhand tobacco smoke and reducing the incentive for smokers to quit (114).

Despite the incontrovertible scientific evidence of the harms of secondhand tobacco smoke, the tobacco industry has referred to such findings as "junk science" in an attempt to discredit them (115). The industry has also used front groups in an attempt to successfully convince some people to resist accepting these findings. Much of the impetus for discrediting scientific studies of the health effects of secondhand tobacco smoke comes from the tobacco industry, which develops and publicizes its own biased research to minimize the harmful effects of secondhand tobacco smoke because it fears that restrictions on smoking will reduce sales and profits (116–

119). The tobacco industry has also resorted to attacks on researchers studying the effects of secondhand tobacco smoke by criticizing their motives or qualifications, even while acknowledging internally the validity of their research findings (120, 121).

Researchers funded by or affiliated with the tobacco industry are nearly 100 times more likely than independent researchers to conclude that secondhand tobacco smoke is not harmful to health (122). Much of the research funded by the tobacco industry is not published in peer-reviewed medical journals, is of poor scientific quality, and should not be used in scientific, legal or policy settings unless its quality has been independently assessed (123). The tobacco industry has even attempted to create its own peer-reviewed medical journals to publish papers on the effects of secondhand tobacco smoke that are favourable to its interests (124). A US federal court has ruled that tobacco industry assertions that secondhand tobacco smoke exposure does not cause disease are "fraudulent" (125).

References

7. Schick S, Glantz S. Philip Morris toxicological experiments with fresh sidestream smoke: more toxic than mainstream smoke. Tobacco Control, 2005,14:396–404.

46. Pierce JP, León M. Effectiveness of smoke-free policies. Lancet Oncology, 2008, 9:614–615.

47. Haw SJ, Gruer L. Changes in exposure of adult non-smokers to secondhand smoke after implementation of smoke-free legislation in Scotland: national cross sectional survey. British Medical Journal, 2007, 335:549.

48. Borland R et al. Protection from environmental tobacco smoke in California. The case for a smoke-free workplace. Journal of the American Medical Association, 1992, 268:749–752.

49. Pickett MS et al. Smoke-free laws and secondhand smoke exposure in US non-smoking adults, 1999–2002. Tobacco Control, 2006, 15:302–307.

50. Mulcahy M et al. Secondhand smoke exposure and risk following the Irish smoking ban: an assessment of salivary cotinine concentrations in hotel workers and air nicotine levels in bars. Tobacco Control, 2005, 14:384–388.

51. Goodman P et al. Effects of the Irish smoking ban on respiratory health of bar workers and air quality in Dublin pubs. American Journal of Respiratory and Critical Care Medicine, 2007, 175:840–845.

52. Bondy SJ et al. Impact of an indoor smoking ban on bar workers' exposure to secondhand smoke. Journal of Occupational and Environmental Medicine, 2009, 51:612–619.

53. Semple S et al. Secondhand smoke levels in Scottish pubs: the effect of smoke-free legislation. Tobacco Control, 2007, 16:127–132.

54. Centers for Disease Control and Prevention (CDC). Reduced secondhand smoke exposure after implementation of a comprehensive statewide smoking ban, New York, June 26, 2003–June 30, 2004. Morbidity and Mortality Weekly Report, 2007, 56:705–708.

55. Fernando D et al. Legislation reduces exposure to second-hand tobacco smoke in New Zealand bars by about 90%. Tobacco Control, 2007, 16:235–238.

56. Heloma A, Jaakkola MS. Four-year follow-up of smoke exposure, attitudes and smoking behaviour following enactment of Finland's national smoke-free work-place law. Addiction, 2003, 98:1111–1117.

57. Building blocks for tobacco control: a handbook. Geneva, World Health Organization, 2004 (http://

www.who.int/entity/tobacco/resources/publications /general/HANDBOOK%20Lowres%20with%20cover.pdf, accessed 13 November 2009).

58. Gan Q et al. Effectiveness of a smoke-free policy in lowering secondhand smoke concentrations in offices in China. Journal of Occupational and Environmental Medicine, 2008, 50:570–575.

59. Cains T et al. Designated "no smoking" areas provide from partial to no protection from environmental tobacco smoke. Tobacco Control, 2004, 13:17–22.

60. Ventilation for acceptable indoor air quality. Atlanta, GA, American Society of Heating, Refrigerating, and Air-Conditioning Engineers, Inc., 2004 (ANSI/ASHRAE Standard 62.1–2004).

61. Environmental tobacco smoke. Position document approved by ASHRAE Board of Directors, 30 June 2005. Atlanta, GA, American Society of Heating, Refrigerating, and Air-Conditioning Engineers, Inc., 2005.

62. Health effects of exposure to environmental tobacco smoke. Sacramento, CA, California Environmental Agency, Office of Environmental Health Hazard Assessment, 1997 (http://www.oehha.org/air/ environmental_tobacco /finalets.html, accessed 13 November 2009).

63. Institute for Health and Consumer Protection. Activity report 2003. Ispra, European Commission Joint Research Centre Directorate-General, 2004 (http:// ihcp.jrc.ec .europa.eu/docs/IHCP_annual_report/ ihcp03.pdf, accessed 13 November 2009).

64. Valente P et al. Exposure to fine and ultrafine particles from secondhand smoke in public places before and after the smoking ban, Italy 2005. Tobacco Control, 2007, 16:312–3.

65. Menzies D et al. Respiratory symptoms, pulmonary function, and markers of inflammation among bar workers before and after a legislative ban on smoking in public places. Journal of the American Medical Association, 2006, 296:1742–1748.

66. Eisner M, Smith A, Blanc P. Bartenders' respiratory health after establishment of smokefree bars and taverns. Journal of the American Medical Association, 1998, 280:1909–1914.

67. Venn A, Britton J. Exposure to secondhand smoke and biomarkers of cardiovascular disease risk in never-smoking adults. Circulation, 2007, 115:990–995.

68. Richiardi L et al. Cardiovascular benefits of smoking regulations: The effect of decreased exposure to passive smoking. Preventive Medicine, 2009, 48:167–172.

69. Pell JP et al. Smoke-free legislation and hospitalizations for acute coronary syndrome. New England Journal of Medicine, 2008, 359:482–491.

70. Bartecchi C et al. Reduction in the incidence of acute myocardial infarction associated with a citywide smoking ordinance. Circulation, 2006, 114:1490–1496.

71. Khuder SA et al. The impact of a smoking ban on hospital admissions for coronary heart disease. Preventive Medicine, 2007, 45:3–8.

72. Sargent RP et al. Reduced incidence of admissions for myocardial infarction associated with public smoking ban: before and after study. British Medical Journal, 2004, 328:977–980.

73. Lemstra M et al. Implications of a public smoking ban. Canadian Journal of Public Health, 2008, 99:62–65.

74. Meyers DG et al. Cardiovascular effect of bans on smoking in public places: a systematic review and meta-analysis. J Am Coll Cardiol, 2009, 29;54:1249–1255.

75. California tobacco control update: the social norm change approach. Sacramento, CA, California Department of Public Health, Tobacco Control Section, 2006 and 2009 (http://www.cdph.ca.gov/programs/ tobacco/Pages/ CTCPPublications.aspx, accessed 27 August 2009).

76. Evans W et al. Do workplace smoking bans reduce smoking? American Economic Review, 1999, 89:728–747.

77. Levy D, Friend K. Clean air laws: a framework for evaluating and improving clean air laws. Journal of Public Health Management and Practice, 2001, 7:87–97.

78. Fichtenberg CM, Glantz SA. Effect of smoke-free work-places on smoking behaviour: systematic review. British Medical Journal, 2002, 325:188.

79. Bauer JE et al. A longitudinal assessment of the impact of smoke-free worksite policies on tobacco use. American Journal of Public Health, 2005, 95:1024–1029.

80. Fong GT et al. Reductions in tobacco smoke pollution and increases in support for smoke-free public places following the implementation of comprehensive smoke-free workplace legislation in the Republic of Ireland: findings from the International Tobacco Control (ITC) Ireland/UK Survey. Tobacco Control, 2006, 15(Suppl. 3):iii51–iii58.

81. Fowkes FJ et al. Scottish smoke-free legislation and trends in smoking cessation. Addiction, 2008, 103:1888–1895.

82. Borland RM et al. Determinants and consequences of smoke-free homes: findings from the International Tobacco Control (ITC) Four Country Survey. Tobacco Control, 2006, 15(Suppl. 3):iii42–iii50.

83. Wipfli H et al. Secondhand smoke exposure among women and children: evidence from 31 countries. American Journal of Public Health 2008, 98:672–679.

84. Borland R et al. Trends in environmental tobacco smoke restrictions in the home in Victoria, Australia. Tobacco Control, 1999, 8:266–271.

85. After the smoke has cleared: evaluation of the impact of a new smokefree law. Wellington, New Zealand Ministry of Health, 2006 (http://www.moh.govt.nz/ moh.nsf/0 /A9D3734516F6757ECC25723D00752D50, accessed 13 November 2009).

86. Evans D, Byrne C. The 2004 Irish smoking ban: is there a "knock-on" effect on smoking in the home? Dublin, Health Service Executive of the Republic of Ireland, Western Area, 2006.

87. Albers AB et al. Household smoking bans and adolescent antismoking attitudes and smoking initiation: findings from a longitudinal study of a Massachusetts youth cohort. American Journal of Public Health, 2008, 98:1886–1893.

88. Li Q et al. Support for smoke free policies among smokers and non-smokers in six cities in China. Tobacco Control, 13 August 2009 (epub ahead of print).

89. Major new poll shows public support across UK for comprehensive smokefree law. London, Action on Smoking and Health, Press Release 30 December 2005 (http:// www.ash.org.uk/ash_jf9oyumi.htm, accessed 18 September 2009).

90. Sebrié EM et al. Smokefree environments in Latin America: on the road to real change? Prevention and Control, 2008, 3:21–35.

91. Equipos Mori. Estudio de "Conocimiento y actitudes hacia el decreto 288/005" (Regulación de consumo de

tabaco en lugares públicos y privados) [Regulation of snuff consumption in public and private places]. Washington, DC, Organización Panamericana de la Salud (Pan American Health Organization), 2006 (http://www.presidencia .gub.uy/_web/ noticias/2006/12/informeo_dec268_mori.pdf, accessed 13 November 2009).

92. Aotearoa New Zealand smokefree workplaces: a 12-month report. Wellington, Asthma and Respiratory Foundation of New Zealand, 2005 (http://www.no-smoke.org /pdf/NZ_TwelveMonthReport.pdf, accessed 13 November 2009).

93. Poll shows 98% of us believe Irish workplaces are healthier as a result of the smokefree law. Naas, Office of Tobacco Control (Press release 28 March 2005; http:// www.otc.ie/article.asp?article=267, accessed 13 November 2009).

94. California bar patrons' Field Research Corporation polls, March 1998 and September 2002. Sacramento, CA, California Department of Public Health, Tobacco Control Section, 2002.

95. China tobacco control report. Beijing, Ministry of Health of the People's Republic of China, 2007.

96. Danishevski K et al. Public attitudes towards smoking and tobacco control policy in Russia. Tobacco Control, 2008, 17:276–283.

97. Scollo M et al. Review of the quality of studies on the economic effects of smoke-free policies on the hospitality industry. Tobacco Control, 2003, 12:13–20.

98. Scollo M, Lal A. Summary of studies assessing the economic impact of smoke-free policies in the hospitality industry. Carlton, VicHealth Centre for Tobacco Control, 2008 (http://www.vctc.org.au/ downloads/Hospitality summary.pdf, accessed 28 August 2009).

99. Borland R et al. Support for and reported compliance with smoke-free restaurants and bars by smokers in four countries: findings from the International Tobacco Control (ITC) Four Country Survey. Tobacco Control, 2006, 15(Suppl. 3):iii34–iii41.

100. Lund M. Smoke-free bars and restaurants in Norway. Oslo, National Institute for Alcohol and Drug Research (SIRUS), 2005 (http://www.sirus.no/internett/tobakk / publication/375.html, accessed 13 November 2009).

101. Edwards R et al. After the smoke has cleared: evaluation of the impact of a new national smoke-free law in New Zealand. Tobacco Control, 2008, 17:e2.

102. Tang H et al. Changes of knowledge, attitudes, beliefs, and preference of bar owner and staff in response to a smoke-free bar law. Tobacco Control, 2004, 13:87–89.

103. The state of smoke-free New York City: a one-year review. New York: New York City Department of Finance, New York City Department of Health & Mental Hygiene, New York City Department of Small Business Services, New York City Economic Development Corporation, 2004. (http://www.nyc.gov/ html/doh/downloads/pdf/smoke /sfaa-2004report.pdf, accessed 28 August 2009).

104. Eriksen M, Chaloupka F. The economic impact of clean indoor air laws. CA: a Cancer Journal for Clinicians, 2007, 57:367–378.

105. Hyland A, Cummings KM. Restaurant employment before and after the New York City Smoke-Free Air Act. Journal of Public Health Management and Practice, 1999, 5:22–27.

106. Alpert HR et al. Environmental and economic evaluation of the Massachusetts Smoke-Free Workplace Law. Journal of Community Health, 2007, 32:269–281.

107. Pyles MK et al. Economic effect of a smoke-free law in a tobacco-growing community. Tobacco Control, 2007, 16:66–68.

108. Dai C et al. The economic impact of Florida's Smoke-Free Workplace Law. Gainesville, FL, University of Florida, Warrington College of Business Administration, Bureau of Economic and Business Research, 2004.

109. Alamar B, Glantz SA. Effect of smoke-free laws on bar value and profits. American Journal of Public Health, 2007, 97:1400–1402.

110. Binkin N et al. Effects of a generalised ban on smoking in bars and restaurants, Italy. International Journal of Tuberculosis and Lung Disease, 2007, 11:522–527.

111. A study of public attitudes toward cigarette smoking and the tobacco industry in 1978, Vol. 1. Storrs: The Roper Organization, 1978 (http://legacy.library.ucsf. edu/tid /qra99d00/pdf, accessed 13 November 2009).

112. Heironimus J. Impact of workplace restrictions on consumption and incidence. Tobacco Documents Online, 1992 (http://tobaccodocuments.org/pm/2023914280 -4284.html, accessed 13 November 2009).

113. Sebrie E, Glantz S. "Accommodating" smoke-free policies: tobacco industry's Courtesy of Choice programme in Latin America. Tobacco Control, 2007, 16:e6.

114. Smoking in public places. House of Commons Health Committee, first report of session 2005–2006, Vol. II. London, House of Commons, 2005 (http://www. publications. parliament.uk/pa/cm200506/cmselect/ cmhealth/485 /485ii.pdf, accessed 13 November 2009).

115. Samet JM, Burke TA. Turning science into junk: the tobacco industry and passive smoking. American Journal of Public Health, 2001, 91:1742–1744.

116. Ong EK, Glantz SA. Tobacco industry efforts subverting International Agency for Research on Cancer's secondhand smoke study. Lancet, 2000, 355:1253–1259.

117. Ong EK, Glantz SA. Constructing "sound science" and "good epidemiology": tobacco, lawyers, and public relations firms. American Journal of Public Health, 2001, 91:1749–1757.

118. Tong EK, Glantz SA. Tobacco industry efforts undermining evidence linking secondhand smoke with cardiovascular disease. Circulation, 2007, 116:1845–1854.

119. Bornhauser A et al. German tobacco industry's successful efforts to maintain scientific and political respectability to prevent regulation of secondhand smoke. Tobacco Control, 2006, 15:e1.

120. Robinson JB. ETS in Nordic countries. Paper presented at: PM EEC ETS Conference, Geneva, 12–14 November 1986. San Francisco, CA, University of California Legacy Tobacco Documents Library, 1986.

121. Tobacco Institute. Embargoed for use in A.M. newspapers, Monday 810615. San Francisco, CA, University of California Legacy Tobacco Documents Library, 1981 (Philip Morris Collection; Bates No. 2015018011/8012; http://legacy. library.ucsf.edu/tid/arl68e00, accessed 13 November 2009).

122. Barnes DE, Bero LA. Why review articles on the health effects of passive smoking reach different conclusions. Journal of the American Medical Association, 1998, 279:1566–1570.

123. Barnes DE, Bero LA. Scientific quality of original research articles on environmental tobacco smoke. Tobacco Control, 1997, 6:19–26.

124. Garne D et al. Environmental tobacco smoke research published in the journal Indoor and Built Environment and associations with the tobacco industry. Lancet, 2005, 365:804–809.

125. United States of America v. Philip Morris USA, Inc., et al., 449 F Supp 2d 1 (2006).

> *"The question now is, how come public health officials can't come out straight and say the reason we're banning smoking on parks and beaches is we want to protect smokers?"*

Smoking Bans Are Misleading

Ronald Bayer, as told to Sarah Clune

In the following viewpoint, Ronald Bayer tells Sarah Clune that public smoking bans are misleading and based on extremely weak evidence. He insists that at beaches and parks, the harm to nonsmokers from cigarette smoke is virtually nonexistent, as is the evidence of discarded cigarette butts killing wildlife and children being encouraged to smoke by seeing adult smokers. The real reason behind these bans is to protect smokers from themselves by making smoking harder, Bayer says, and health officials use other arguments to not appear paternalistic. In fact, he continues, public smoking bans are effective in "denormalizing" smoking and increasing quit rates. Bayer is a professor of sociomedical sciences at Columbia University's Mailman School of Public Health. Clune is a former producer at PBS NewsHour.

As you read, consider the following questions:

1. Why did public smoking bans start to take effect, according to Bayer?

2. What is Bayer's stance on the "nanny state's" smoking bans?

3. What do health officials risk by making claims based on weak evidence, as stated by Bayer?

Summer has officially begun and for many, it's time for sun, sand and swimming. But don't count on lighting up a cigarette while you're at the beach.

Over the last few years, you may have noticed more "no smoking" signs have cropped up on parks and beaches. They're part of a larger trend banning smoking at outside, public areas. In fact, smoking has been banned in 843 parks and more than 150 beaches in the last two decades.

What beachgoers probably aren't thinking about is the ethics behind these bans, which began taking hold in the early 1990s.

Public health officials have long argued the bans are meant to eliminate dangers from secondhand, or "sidestream smoke," reduce the environmental impact of cigarette butts and to keep young, impressionable children from picking up on bad habits. Makes sense, right?

But a new article in this month's [July 2013's] *Health Affairs* looks at the shockingly slim evidence behind these bans.

"I discovered the evidence was really weak," explained lead author Ronald Bayer, a professor at Columbia University's Mailman School of Public Health. "The evidence of harm to nonsmokers on the beach or in a park from someone smoking is virtually nonexistent."

Bayer points out that there is, however, an important public health benefit from such bans. "They make it more difficult for smokers to smoke," Bayer told us, "and contribute in an important way to the 'denormalization' of smoking."

Bayer joined *PBS NewsHour* late last week to discuss the new study and the potential risks the rationale behind these bans have on future public health initiatives.

Tightening of the Tobacco Control Movement

PBS NewsHour: Ronald Bayer, thank you for joining us. This is an interesting ethical question to look into. What started you down this road?

Ronald Bayer, Columbia University Mailman School of Public Health: I noticed when my students of public health talked about illicit drugs like heroin or cocaine or marijuana, they adopted a libertarian point of view—emphasizing how the government has no business intruding on people's choices and all those negative consequences. But when I raised the issue of tobacco, they all became in a way, authoritarian. "We have to limit smoking, we have to limit where people smoke, we have to protect people from themselves, we have to protect their children." I was struck by the difference. And I asked my students, "How come when you talk about the other drugs, you adopt sort of a hands-off position, but when you talk about tobacco, you believe the government should intrude more?" I listened to them, and I took their lead in a way, and I said, this was very interesting—what explains this?

PBS NewsHour: Let's take a step back: why, and when, did these bans start taking effect?

Bayer: They really began in earnest in the early 1990s, so it's part in parcel of the tightening of the tobacco control movement, the recognition that we have to do more because several hundred people die each year from tobacco-related diseases. I looked at the arguments for why we had to ban smoking in parks and beaches, and there were three—and they were really very striking.

One was that smoking is dangerous to people around the smoker. So, it's one thing if a smoker wants to smoke, it's his or her business, but as one tobacco control advocate said, if you can smell it, it may be killing you. We're familiar with the secondhand smoke argument—that's what happens if you ban smoking in a bar, or a restaurant. But the beach or a park is a very different location. It's open, the air is open. So what is the risk? And the public health people said, we don't know the exact risk, but there is a risk, and it's unacceptable.

The second argument was that tobacco butts endanger wildlife, because they get washed into the sea and fish and birds consume these butts and it kills them. Or, cigarette butts represent the kind of revolting litter on beaches, and to prove that, people involved in environmental control would actually count the number of cigarette butts they found on a beach and there are billions and billions of those, as you can imagine.

The third argument, and the most interesting argument to me, was that parents and families have the right to take their kids to the beach, or a park, without seeing anyone smoke. It's like bad behavior, just the way we want to protect our kids from hearing people curse, or get drunk; we don't want them to see smokers because maybe they'll emulate it.

The Evidence Is Extremely Weak

PBS NewsHour: And do these arguments pan out?

Bayer: I discovered the evidence was really weak. The evidence of harm to nonsmokers on the beach or in a park from someone smoking is virtually nonexistent. The evidence that fish and birds are dying because of cigarette butts is virtually nonexistent. And even the evidence that seeing someone in a park or beach will encourage kids to smoke is extremely weak.

So I said to myself, what's going on here? What's the public health impulse that's involved that leads to these bans if the evidence is so weak? Because everyone in public health believes that what we do should be evidence based.

As I thought about it, it became very clear that what was involved wasn't that we were trying to protect nonsmokers from sidestream smoke on parks and beaches. We weren't really concerned about birds and fish. There wasn't really evidence that we were going to protect kids by disallowing smoking in parks and beaches.

What was involved was that we really wanted to make it less and less possible for people to smoke, because it's bad for them and we're trying to protect smokers themselves from a behavior that's going to increase the risk of disease and death.

A Kind of Nanny State

PBS NewsHour: So, why did public health officials base their case on this weak evidence?

Bayer: The question now is, how come public health officials can't come out straight and say the reason we're banning smoking on parks and beaches is we want to protect smokers? We want to get them to give it up, we want them to smoke less and we want to make it more difficult for people to begin smoking.

I think it's because public health officials don't want to be tarred with the brush of the "nanny state," of "Big Brother." In the United States, it's the same story of the motorcycle helmets. When we tried to impose motorcycle helmet laws in the United States, we made all kinds of arguments about how when a person gets into an accident, they really cost us all money because they have to go to emergency rooms and we have to pay for it. That's not why we wanted motorcycle helmet laws. We wanted motorcycle helmet laws because we wanted to protect motorcyclists against their stupid behavior. We couldn't say it, because that sounds like we're finger wagging.

Nonsmoking Regulations as Segregation Measures

As a result of such ambitious attempts to establish that environmental tobacco smoke is nearly as dangerous as the smoking of cigarettes, the conclusion is drawn that exposure is to be avoided like the plague or leprosy. Aside from being a smelly annoyance, tobacco smoke has become demonized into something that is likely to inflict serious harm 'within minutes'. Day after day, more and more local authorities issue more stringent nonsmoking regulations as a result of which smokers become effectively zoned out of public spaces and relegated to spots that serve both as pillories and asylums.

In a democracy, such regulations have a self-reinforcing effect. The fewer people smoke the more support is garnered for segregation measures by the large majority. Segregation measures, in turn, reinforce the social force of the norm they enforce. They have a normalizing effect. The uncontaminated environment becomes the norm. 'Smoke-free' has come to designate quality for establishments just as 'judenfrei' was the accomplishment villages in Austria prided themselves on during the Nazi period.

Alexander Somek, Individualism: An Essay on the Authority of the European Union. *New York: Oxford University Press, 2008, p. 56.*

PBS NewsHour: So are these cigarette bans that same type of finger wagging?

Bayer: I actually think these bans on parks and beaches represent, I think, a kind of paternalism, a kind of nanny state. The question is, is the nanny state so wrong? If we could eliminate 400,000 deaths a year over time because fewer and fewer people smoke, would that be so bad? And I think not. But I think public health officials are afraid to make the case that directly, so they get caught in making a case that, I think, is easily picked apart.

PBS NewsHour: Have these bans proven effective? Is there any link between more of these bans and lower smoking rates, or healthier populations?

Bayer: That's a good question, and actually, the evidence is still weak. It's not clear.

But it is clear that the general process of denormalizing smoking has an effect. It has an effect on quit rates and it has an effect on start rates. So that as part of a broader campaign to denormalize—to take something that was normal, social behavior, and to turn it into something a little weird, a little off—(it) does in fact have an impact, as do taxing tobacco products.

Honesty Is the Best Policy for Public Health

PBS NewsHour: In your conclusion, you state, "Public health must, in the end, rely on public trust." Was there a risk that public health officials took justifying these bans the way they did?

Bayer: Well, I actually do think there's a risk. My concern is that when public health officials make claims that can't be backed by the evidence, they run the risk of people saying, "We can't trust you." I understand it is probably more effective to say the reason we're banning smoking on parks and beaches is that we're protecting you from sidestream smoke, or your kids from looking at something very bad for them or that we're protecting wildlife. That might be a more effective way in the short run of getting these statutes or regulations passed and put into place.

But in the long run, I think, that if people begin to feel that they're being toyed with, that the evidence is not being presented in a straightforward way, it's going to backfire. I think the evidence in the arguments made to implement these bans is absent, and in some of the cases, very weak.

PBS NewsHour: So, public health officials should just be more honest?

Bayer: In a crude way, honesty may be a more difficult policy, but I think it is in fact the best policy for public health.

PBS NewsHour: Ronald Bayer, thanks for joining us.

Bayer: Thanks for having me.

| "It's clear that raising the smoking age
| would have massive health benefits."

Raise the Smoking Age to 21

John Kruzel

In the following viewpoint, John Kruzel writes that raising the smoking age from eighteen to twenty-one would reduce youth smoking and benefit public health. The recent law passed in New York City is inspired by the success of Needham, Massachusetts, which has a 56 percent lower adult smoking rate than the entire state of Massachusetts since enacting its law in 2005, Kruzel says. Also, people aged eighteen to twenty purchase 90 percent of cigarettes on behalf of minors, he points out, and a higher smoking age would cut younger teens off. Nonetheless, the author criticizes the federal government for ignoring the evidence and urges it to persuade states to follow New York City's example. Kruzel is a contributor to Slate *and a law student in Washington, DC.*

As you read, consider the following questions:

1. Who first argued for raising the smoking age to twenty-one, as told by Kruzel?

2. Why does the author encourage the White House to explore the health benefits of a higher tobacco sales age?

3. What examples does the author provide to support his claim that the Barack Obama administration is not following the June 2014 deadline of the Family Smoking Prevention and Tobacco Control Act?

The [Barack] Obama administration is facing a health care deadline. I'm not referring to the White House's self-imposed target date to unsuck healthcare.gov. I mean that the administration has until summer 2014 to advise Congress of the health benefits of raising the age of tobacco sales from 18 years old to 21. In the meantime, there's a mini-movement afoot in several municipalities to tighten restrictions. It's clear that raising the smoking age would have massive health benefits. Congress should consolidate this momentum into a nationwide regulation that lifts the minimum sales age to 21.

New York City offers the highest-profile example of a city's legislative efforts to stop young people from getting hooked on tobacco. Last month [in October 2013] the City Council approved legislation that raised the minimum legal sales age from 18 to 21. It will take effect six months after garnering a mayoral signature. There's a similar bill before the Washington, D.C.'s council, and Hawaii and New Jersey are expected to soon consider statewide legislation.

The authors of both the New York City and Washington, D.C., bills specifically cite the success of Needham, Mass., as a source of inspiration. The Boston suburb enacted a regulation in 2005 barring anyone under 21 from buying tobacco products. Since then, the adult smoking rate in Needham has been shown to be fully 56 percent lower than the overall rate in Massachusetts, according to recent findings by the Massachusetts Department of Public Health. In part, local officials attribute the lower smoking rate and its corollary health benefits—lower mortality rates and fewer hospitalizations due to lung cancer—to the decision to raise the age for tobacco purchases to 21.

Every day in America, about 4,000 people under 18 smoke their first cigarette, and 1,000 go on to become daily cigarette smokers. Most adolescents who have smoked more than 100 cigarettes have reported that they'd like to quit but can't. So perhaps it's not surprising that one of the most persuasive arguments for raising the minimum sales age came from a high schooler.

Cutting Off Cigarettes Purchased for Minors

Prompted by an essay contest about how to change the world, then 17-year-old Jessica Adelson argued for increasing the age for tobacco sales from 18 to 21. In 2007, the teenage Adelson appeared before the state legislature in her home state of Connecticut. "By increasing the age, we can stop many young people from getting their hands on cigarettes," she told lawmakers. According to the AP [Associated Press], Adelson further testified that "younger teens typically know a lot more 18-year-olds than 21-year-olds who might buy them cigarettes." Adelson's argument is borne out by the authors of a recent article in the *Annals of Internal Medicine*, who write that people aged 18–20 are responsible for 90 percent of the cigarettes purchased on behalf of minors. Cut them off, and the benefits would extend down to much younger teens.

But the 18–20 set does more than just supply cigarettes to underage smokers. According to a mix of firm statistics, anecdata [anecdotal data], and a damning confession by a Big Tobacco official, this age group also gets addicted to nicotine in big numbers. "A significant number do in fact start between 18 and 21," John Banzhaf, the executive director of Action on Smoking and Health, told CNN in 2002. Among 18- to 25-

year-olds, the average age of first use is 18.9 years old, according to cardiologist Mehmet Oz.

On the retail side, one New York City vendor told a local CBS affiliate that half of his cigarette sales go to people between the ages of 18 and 21. But perhaps the most damning line (and maybe the obvious causal explanation) comes from a 1982 internal memo penned by an employee of the tobacco manufacturer R.J. Reynolds: "If a man has never smoked by age 18, the odds are three-to-one he never will. By age 24, the odds are twenty-to-one." To put it another way, in the words of Patrick Reynolds, the grandson of R.J. Reynolds who would spurn the family trade to become an antismoking advocate, "Once they reach 21, it's no longer an interesting vehicle for rebellion."

It's tempting to point to the Needham, Mass., statistics and other data as ironclad proof that raising the age of tobacco sales across America would lead to a national health bonanza. While the findings represent a promising first step in substantiating such a proposition, the empirical data lack the depth and breadth necessary to overcome the backlash from Big Tobacco that a national push would provoke. This is where the White House could make itself useful by exploring the health benefits of a higher tobacco sales age—especially considering the Obama administration is required by law to do exactly this.

The Obstruction of Federal Government Inertia

In 2009, when Congress passed the Family Smoking Prevention and Tobacco Control Act, which allowed the FDA [US Food and Drug Administration] to regulate certain aspects of tobacco sales, advertising and use, lawmakers also gave the administration a June 2014 deadline. "The Secretary of Health and Human Services shall . . . convene an expert panel to con-

The Health Implications of Delaying Smoking Initiation

Although changing the legal smoking age is likely to prevent initiation in some youth, in others, it may simply delay initiation. This too would have population health implications because there is evidence that people who start smoking in their teens are more likely to become lifelong addicted smokers than those who start later in life. Studies have shown that smoking is a long-term addiction. The median cessation age for those who start smoking as adolescents is 33 years for males and 37 years for females. Moreover, smokers who initiate later in life are more likely to quit.

Sajjad Ahmad,
"The Cost-Effectiveness of Raising the Legal Smoking Age in California," Medical Decision Making, *May–June 2005.*

duct a study on the public health implications of raising the minimum age to purchase tobacco products; and . . . not . . . later than 5 years after the date of enactment of this Act, submit a report to the Congress on the results of such study." But according to Chris Bostic, the deputy director of policy at Action on Smoking and Health, the administration has yet to convene the expert panel mandated under the 2009 statute. Astonishingly, an 899-page report published by the Department of Health and Human Services three years after the law's passage fails to even mention the Needham, Mass., statistics that have catalyzed New York City and the nation's capital to act, and sheds no light on the correlation between a higher tobacco sales age and improved health, as Congress requested. "I wouldn't be surprised if they wait until the last minute," Bostic told me.

The Obama administration has no excuse for dragging its feet over the past four and a half years, particularly after the president trumpeted the Family Smoking Prevention and Tobacco Control Act as a vehicle to protect American youth. It's hard to imagine the Obama administration could do anything besides adding momentum to this growing municipal movement if it simply followed its congressional mandate to explore the nexus between higher tobacco sales ages and health benefits. Given that Congress has already demonstrated its ability to persuade states to set the age of alcohol sales at 21, and that it's capable of producing a similar scheme for tobacco sales, the main obstruction to a nationwide movement with political traction should not be federal government inertia.

"Raising the age from 18 to 21 won't make as big of a difference as lawmakers hope."

Raising the Smoking Age to 21 Is Pointless

Eric Levenson

Eric Levenson is an editorial fellow at the Atlantic Wire. In the following viewpoint, Levenson declares that raising the smoking age from eighteen to twenty-one will fail to make an impact. Smoking rates are already declining due to other smoking policies, he says, including cigarette taxes and smoking bans at workplaces and bars. Moreover, the three-year increase would be ineffective because smokers start at a much earlier age and the restrictions are not always enforced, Levenson argues. As for the success story of the twenty-one smoking age in Needham, Massachusetts, other antismoking laws helped to reduce the city's smoking rate as well, he persists.

As you read, consider the following questions:

1. What figures does the author cite to support his position that smoking is already trending down?

2. As stated by the author, what illegal activities may raising the smoking age make more desirable?

3. Why is raising the smoking age a "tough sell" in the country, as told by the author?

Lawmakers across the country are jumping on the bandwagon to raise the minimum age for smokers, but the odds are that these won't do much to keep kids from lighting up.

Last week [in November 2013], Utah legislators agreed to put a bill on ballots next year that would make 21 the minimum age for buying tobacco products, a raise from its current limit of 19 years, which is already the highest age in the U.S. That plan comes fresh off the passage of New York City's recent rule to raise its minimum age to 21, and similar age-raise plans are soon hitting legislators in Hawaii, New Jersey, Colorado, and Texas.

The underlying reason behind this growing trend is admirable—smoking is bad, duh—but raising the smoking age to 21 would actually make less of an impact than officials think. That's because smoking rates are already coming down, and smokers start way before age 21 anyway.

Smoking Is Already Trending Down

Prior to this trend of raising the age to 21, the smoking rate was already decreasing these past few years, as the CDC [Centers for Disease Control and Prevention] graph to the right shows [not shown]. Last year, 18 percent of Americans smoked, down from about 21 percent in 2009, and almost 25 percent in 1997. This decline isn't due to age raises, but to other smoking laws, including cigarette taxes and smoke-free workplace rules. Similarly, heavy smokers are smoking less, as the CDC reports that those smoking 30 or more cigarettes a day declined significantly from 2005 to 2010. In New York City (where nearly all indoor smoking is banned), the smoking rate sits at 15 percent, down from its 21 percent in 2005. Because of a decreased public visibility and higher cigarette prices, smoking is on the way out. But age limits, which are only now being put in place, have little to do with it.

Smokers Start at Way Younger Age

Raising the age from 18 to 21 won't make as big of a difference as lawmakers hope, given that most smokers—nine out of 10 according to the surgeon general—have already begun lighting up by 18. In Utah, the average age at which a person tries their first cigarette is a prepubescent 12.6 years, according to Cameron Mitchell, the executive director of the Utah Association of Local Health Departments. *Slate*'s argument in favor of raising the smoking age cites an old internal memo from tobacco company R.J. Reynolds: "If a man has never smoked by age 18, the odds are three-to-one he never will." But as the stats above show, most smokers have lit up well before age 18, so those extra three years are unlikely to tip the balance.

More Laws Don't Always Equal More Enforcement

Those numbers above, plus the prevalence of college-age drinkers who have no problem getting their hands on alcohol, suggest that those who want to smoke will have no problem getting their hands on tobacco. This age raise might just make fake IDs and black market cigarettes even more desirable.

Mixed Success of Raising Smoking Ages

Utah's and New York City's role model for this change is Needham, Massachusetts, which raised its smoking age to 21 in 2005 and has seen a large drop in smoking compared to the rest of Massachusetts. Needham's director of public health told WNYC that teen smoking declined from 13.5 percent in 2006 to 5.5 percent in 2012. The Boston suburb's success is impressive, but the same health director is willing to emphasize the city's other antismoking laws aside from just the age raise. "I wouldn't say it's all because of this," she told WNYC. "But I think the community has embraced this." However, Needham's success story hasn't been seen in other age-raising initiatives. Alabama and Alaska raised their minimums to 19 recently, but neither has seen much of a difference yet in their above-average smoking rates.

Utah Has Few Smokers to Be Angry

Utah is the state least in need of a change in its smoking laws. It already has the lowest rate of smoking in the country; just 9.1% in 2010 according to the Centers for Disease Control [and Prevention]. A Gallup poll in 2011, too, put Utah's lowest smoking rate at 11 percent, well below the U.S. average of 21 percent. Because of those small numbers, there likely won't be much opposition to the ballot vote next year. But that can't be said of other states with higher smoking rates, particularly those with a libertarian bent. Consider Kentucky and its 29 percent smoking rate (Gallup) or West Virginia and its 27 percent rate (CDC). Aligning an anti–Big Government campaign with angry young smokers could stop this trend in its tracks.

On top of these reasons, there's also the problem of reconciling a country that can send its 18-year-olds off to war . . . where they can't smoke or drink. That's a tough sell, no matter that officials have their minds in the right place.

Periodical and Internet Sources Bibliography

The following articles have been selected to supplement the diverse views presented in this chapter.

Associated Press	"Outdoor Smoking Bans Double in U.S. Past 5 Years," *CBS News*, August 8, 2013.
Lyle Beckwith	"Cigarette Tax Hikes Don't Help: Opposing View," *USA Today*, March 28, 2013.
Michelle Castillo	"Tripling Cigarette Tax Could Prevent 200 Million Deaths This Century: Study," *CBS News*, January 2, 2014.
Dennis Cauchon	"Tax Hike Cuts Tobacco Consumption," *USA Today*, September 13, 2012.
Melanie Dostis	"In Wake of NYC Bill, Views Split on Tobacco Age," *USA Today*, November 7, 2013.
Geoffrey Kabat	"The Real Motivation Behind Park and Beach Smoking Bans," *Forbes*, July 22, 2013.
Stephanie Nebehey	"Tobacco Taxes, Smoking Bans Set to Save Millions of Lives: Study," *Reuters*, June 30, 2013.
Clara Ritger	"Antismoking Policies Have Saved More than 8 Million Lives," *National Journal Daily*, January 9, 2014.
Andrew Seidman	"Lawmakers Want to Snuff Out Smoking in N.J. Parks, Beaches," *Philadelphia Inquirer*, February 22, 2014.
Alex Swoyer	"U.N. Approves Increased Global Tobacco Tax During Secret Session," *Washington Times*, October 14, 2014.
Leslie Wade	"Doctors Support Raising the Smoking Age," *CNN*, August 26, 2013.

OPPOSING
VIEWPOINTS®
SERIES

CHAPTER 3

How Should Smoking Alternatives Be Regulated?

Chapter Preface

Originally created in Sweden, snus is smokeless tobacco in a moist powder form that has been fermented and comes in packets that resemble tea bags. The user places snus between the upper lip and gums for several minutes or up to several hours. This differs from chewing tobacco, which is held in the lower jaw. Some American tobacco brands, including Camel and Marlboro, manufacture their own versions of snus. In 2012 domestic sales of snus reached $175 million, growing approximately 9 percent a year.

Stricter regulation of snus is being called for in the United States because of its reported dangers. "Although research is ongoing on the health effects of noncombustible tobacco products such as snus," states the Tobacco Control Legal Consortium, "smokeless tobacco products have been shown to cause oral, pancreatic, and esophageal cancers, precancerous mouth lesions, and dental problems." Therefore, the consortium proposes limiting snus's access and appeal to youths, such as urging states and localities to amend, if necessary, existing definitions of "tobacco products" to ensure that snus is comparably taxed to cigarettes and prohibiting the product to be available in fruit and mint flavors.

In arguments against stricter regulation, however, snus is touted as much less harmful than smoking. Speaking of the total ban on snus in the European Union (except for Sweden), Clive Bates, trustee at the Transform Drug Policy Foundation in London, England, argues that "given the addictiveness of nicotine and how difficult some smokers find quitting even if they really want to, banning this option amounts to death by regulation." Bates insists that the smokeless tobacco product has benefited public health in the Scandinavian country. "Sweden has by far the lowest level of tobacco-related mortality in the developed world, the lowest rate of smoking and the highest use of tobacco in smokeless form," he maintains. In the following chapter, the authors debate how alternatives to smoking should be regulated.

> *"Regulation would prevent tobacco companies from adopting their usual cynical and devious tactics to hook young people to a product that serves as a gateway to their main business interest—the sale of regular cigarettes."*

Time for E-Cigarette Regulation

Lancet Oncology

The Lancet Oncology *is a specialized medical journal. In the following viewpoint, the journal calls for the federal regulation of electronic cigarettes, or e-cigarettes. As unregulated products, e-cigarettes are being aggressively marketed and freely promoted to young consumers, argues the* Lancet Oncology. *Users are likely to seek higher dosages of nicotine and eventually smoke regular cigarettes, the journal adds. Thus, e-cigarettes should be regulated as medical devices to help people quit smoking, advises the* Lancet Oncology, *before the tobacco industry uses them to hook new smokers.*

As you read, consider the following questions:

1. In what ways are e-cigarettes being marketed to a younger target audience, as alleged by the *Lancet Oncology?*

2. In the *Lancet Oncology*'s view, why is it ironic that tobacco companies are moving into the e-cigarette market?

3. Why do e-cigarettes pose a danger of normalizing smoking, as argued by the *Lancet Oncology*?

The increasing use of e-cigarettes has been cautiously welcomed by health advocates. The hope is that these devices offer a safe means to deliver nicotine without the array of carcinogenic compounds found in cigarettes. However, there is increasing disquiet over the disconnect between these health objectives and the way in which e-cigarettes are being advertised. Most importantly, new evidence released by the US Centers for Disease Control and Prevention (CDC) on Sept 6, 2013, shows that use of e-cigarettes by children and teenagers has more than doubled in the past 2 years. There is a real danger of the devices becoming a gateway product, attracting more young people to begin smoking, undoing years of public awareness campaigning on the dangers of smoking.

The safety of e-cigarettes versus regular cigarettes is an ongoing debate. Certainly, smokeless inhalation systems do not have many of the carcinogenic compounds present in traditional cigarettes. Some evidence also exists that e-cigarettes are as effective in helping smokers quit as are other nicotine delivery devices, such as nicotine patches. However, in the USA, a legal case between Sottera (an importer and distributor of e-cigarettes) and the US Food and Drug Administration ruled that e-cigarettes should be regulated as "tobacco products" unless explicitly marketed for therapeutic purposes.

While this legal wrangling continues, the range of available e-cigarettes continues to expand, and they are not being advertised as smoking cessation devices. Instead they are being marketed aggressively as lifestyle-choice consumables. By contrast with traditional cigarette advertising—outlawed in many

Vaping and Public Places

Many smoke-free laws define the act of "smoking" as inhaling or carrying a lighted tobacco or plant product intended for inhalation. E-cigarettes, which are not burned, but "vaped," are generally not covered under these laws. Using e-cigarettes in public may lead conventional smokers to assume that smoking is permitted in such locations and nonsmokers to believe that a smoke-free law is being violated. Because of this, several health organizations recommend that the use of electronic cigarettes be prohibited in public places and workplaces.

Tobacco Control Legal Consortium,
"Regulatory Options for Electronic Cigarettes," February 2013.

countries—e-cigarettes can be advertised via any medium. Increasingly, this takes the form of prominent sponsorship deals. In the USA, blu eCigs sponsors an IndyCar team, while in the UK, Merthyr Town Football Club has renamed its stadium the Cigg-e Stadium in light of a sponsorship deal, and E-lites have gone into partnership with Scottish football team Celtic.

Most disturbingly, these promotions will attract the attention of younger consumers, as will other aspects of e-cigarettes' marketing. Indeed, e-cigarettes are currently available in flavours that read like the contents of a sweetshop—bubblegum, chocolate, and popcorn are just some on offer. Further, e-cigarette companies are actively soliciting their consumers to become brand managers to promote their products through social media—a cynical attempt to appeal to a younger target audience. These promotional tactics are working. Tom Frieden, director of the CDC, commented: "The increased use of e-cigarettes by teens is deeply troubling. Nicotine is a highly addictive drug. Many teens who start with e-cigarettes may be condemned to struggling with a lifelong addiction to nicotine and conventional cigarettes."

The addictive nature of nicotine is where the inherent flaw in e-cigarette advocacy lies. Irrespective of the safety of the delivery mechanism, regular use of addictive substances causes users to become acclimatised to their current dosage and seek other ways to increase it. With nicotine, this will most probably lead to use of traditional cigarettes. It is telling that major tobacco companies are increasingly moving into the e-cigarette market through the purchase of small, independent companies. For example, according to the 2012 annual report of US tobacco firm Lorillard, blu eCigs accounted for most of their 4.2% growth last year, and British American Tobacco recently acquired e-cigarette company Vype to expand their portfolio of products. Thus we find ourselves in an ironic position where tobacco companies are manufacturing devices that are being touted as aids to smoking cessation.

Finally, e-cigarettes also pose a serious danger of renormalising smoking. Given that most e-cigarettes are designed to mimic cigarettes in as many ways as possible, being around people lighting up—electronically or otherwise—will once again become socially acceptable. Tireless campaigning has drawn attention to the dangers of secondhand smoke to others; the normalisation of e-cigarettes will confuse those efforts.

E-cigarettes may yet prove to be an effective way of delivering nicotine safely and a means by which some people can quit their addiction. But in their present unregulated state, manufacturers are free to promote the devices in any way they choose. E-cigarettes should be regulated as medical devices, and their promotion should come under the ordinance of the WHO [World Health Organization] Framework Convention on Tobacco Control. Such regulation would prevent tobacco companies from adopting their usual cynical and devious tactics to hook young people to a product that serves as a gateway to their main business interest—the sale of regular cigarettes.

> *"Effectively excluding e-cigarettes from the market via stringent regulation would have the effect of killing smokers and protecting cigarette and pharmaceutical markets."*

Smoking Kills, and So Might E-Cigarette Regulation

Gilbert Ross

In the following viewpoint, Gilbert Ross argues that strict federal regulation of electronic cigarettes, or e-cigarettes, threatens the potential for the technology to help smokers quit. With fewer harmful ingredients and no combustion, the devices are very likely to be safer than conventional cigarettes and a promising cessation treatment, he says. However, if the US Food and Drug Administration (FDA) designates e-cigarettes as tobacco products that require proof of modified risk, Ross maintains, they would be removed from the market for lengthy testing, leaving smokers to revert to deadly cigarettes and benefiting the tobacco industry. The author is medical and executive director of the American Council on Science and Health.

As you read, consider the following questions:

1. Why do current nicotine replacement therapies provide an unacceptably low level of assistance in smoking cessation, as explained by Ross?

2. How would the tobacco industry profit from regulating e-cigarettes, in Ross's view?

3. What approach does Ross recommend instead of stringently regulating e-cigarettes?

Anyone with a modicum of knowledge regarding public health will agree that the most important, devastating, and preventable issue facing America is the human toll of cigarettes. Yet our nation's main health regulator, the Food and Drug Administration (FDA), will issue regulations within the next few weeks [in late 2013] that could harm our nation's 45 million smokers.

Smokers trying to quit have an extremely difficult time, yet a new technology which might ease their path—electronic cigarettes, or e-cigarettes—is facing relentless opposition from public health agencies such as the Centers for Disease Control [and Prevention], the FDA, and the American Cancer Society (which sponsors this week's Great American Smokeout to encourage quitting)—and their antipathy is certainly not based on science.

We do not yet know what the long-term health effects of e-cigarettes are, nor the benefits for smokers who switch or cut down on their daily quota of smokes via "vaping" (using e-cigarettes) since there is no smoke involved. But simple common sense would dictate that inhaling the fewer, less harmful ingredients of e-cigarettes as compared to inhaling the thousands of chemicals in the smoke from burnt tobacco, many of which have been shown to be carcinogenic, is highly likely to be healthier.

A tragic 450,000 Americans die from smoking each year. While the fraction of adult smokers has been in gradual decline since the groundbreaking 1964 surgeon general's report confirmed the evidence of manifold smoking-related illnesses, the total number has not changed much and the decline in teen smoking initiation has stalled over the past few years. Although "cigarette smoke" is not listed as a cause of death per se, smokers whose lives are cut short die from a wide spectrum of illnesses, some chronic (cancers of many organs, COPD/chronic obstructive pulmonary disease), and some cruelly brief (heart attacks and strokes). If those who die prematurely from smoking were lumped together, they would constitute the third leading cause of death in America, after heart disease and cancer.

Most smokers understandably desire to quit. About half try each year, but a pitiful few—maybe 5 percent—succeed unaided or "cold turkey." The addiction to smoking is extremely powerful, largely (but not solely) due to nicotine's power. However, it is often believed by smokers, and even by some doctors, that it is the nicotine that is toxic and lethal. This is a dangerous myth. It has been proven that smokers smoke for the nicotine—but they die from the smoke. The FDA has approved various treatments to help smokers quit— NRT (nicotine replacement therapy) patches, gum, inhalers, and non-nicotine drugs such as bupropion and varenicline (Zyban and Chantix, respectively). The unfortunate fact is that adding one or more of these treatments to a smoker's stated desire to quit increases his or her success rate—abstinence from cigarettes for one year—by about two- to three-fold, i.e., to 15 percent or less. These methods, which fail almost 9 times out of 10, provide an unacceptably low level of assistance in aiding escape from smoking's deadly grip.

Over the course of the past few years, e-cigarettes (or "electronic nicotine delivery systems," ENDS) have provided a ray of hope for an increasing number of desperate smokers.

These devices use a battery to vaporize water and nicotine, which the user ("vaper") inhales, along with vegetable glycerin and/or propylene glycol and flavoring. They often have a cigarette-like LED tip which glows red, or some other color if preferred, but without tobacco, without combustion, and without smoke. The ingredients noted are generally recognized as safe by regulatory agencies, and have been in common use for decades—although no long-term health studies have been done on their safety in combination with inhalational use.

Since 2007, when e-cigarettes were first imported from China, smokers have at first gradually, and more recently enthusiastically, become vapers. Solid data on long-term trends are only beginning to be accumulated, but the sales of e-cigarettes have doubled in each of the past few years, to the extent that a recent survey found that an astounding one-fifth of smokers had tried them—millions of people, in other words. How many have switched completely from deadly cigarettes? How many smokers also vape—"dual users"? None of this has been determined yet by randomized clinical trials. Although there are scant data even from observational studies, several small studies support the contention that vaping is likely to be more effective than NRT for smoking cessation, as well as for reducing the number of cigarettes smoked among those who have not yet quit.

The Upcoming FDA Decision

The Family Smoking Prevention and Tobacco Control Act, which granted the FDA oversight of tobacco in 2009, outlines a complex process for "modified risk tobacco products" (MRTPs) to be approved by the FDA. Such a product must undergo a lengthy and expensive trial process requiring demonstration that the product submitted reduces the harm of tobacco exposure not merely for the person using it, but for the population as a whole. Given the nefarious behavior of the to-

Neither Nicotine nor Tobacco

Citing the ambiguity and confusion surrounding the regulatory and legal status of electronic cigarettes, Ruyan America Inc. has reformulated and renamed its product. The company now offers the Ruyan Rapp E-mystic (pronounced "ee mist-stick") a product that contains an established dietary supplement/herbal remedy—lobelia—rather than nicotine. "It tested extremely well in focus groups," says Bill Bartkowski, president of Ruyan America. The product contains neither nicotine nor tobacco and is being marketed under the Dietary Supplement Health and Education Act of 1994, incurring fewer regulatory concerns than nicotine, says Bartkowski.

Troutman Sanders Tobacco Team,
"Classifying Electronic Cigarettes," Smokeshop, *February 2010.*

bacco industry over the 20th century, any proposal submitted to the FDA related to tobacco is going to have to strongly support any assertions with data.

Unfortunately, the Tobacco Control Act may become a detriment to public health if it is implemented to effectively ban e-cigarettes from the market. The Office of Management and Budget is currently deciding whether to designate e-cigarettes as a tobacco product to be regulated under the TCA, as a drug or medical device, requiring regulation from a different department of the FDA, or as neither such product. If e-cigarettes are designated as tobacco products requiring proof of modified risk, it is likely that the ramifications for millions of American vapers, and many more potential future ex-smokers, will be disastrous. E-cigarettes (at least those containing the nicotine smokers crave) would be exiled from the market while expensive, lengthy testing took place. Ironically, the industry's small businesses would suffer while Big Tobacco would profit, since it has also gotten into the e-cigarette market, and since larger companies would be the only ones who could afford to cut through the regulatory thicket. Meanwhile, some ex-smokers who have become vapers will find a way to secure their e-cigarette nicotine, via online or black market sources. Many, however, will revert to the deadly, toxic cigarettes from which they thought they had, at last, escaped.

There is, however, a better approach: The government could decline to classify e-cigarettes as tobacco products and allow their continued marketing, with the states establishing reasonable oversight—as many have already—for age limits, manufacturing standards, accurate ingredient listing, and warning labels. As a result, many lives will be saved from cigarette-related disease and death.

The World Health Organization predicts that the death toll from cigarettes could reach 1 billion this century, if current trends continue. The European Union only last month flouted the anti-e-cigarette campaigners and gave millions of European vapers a pass to keep on vaping. Given the current abysmal rate of successful quitting with the approved methods, the FDA should take the courageous, science-based, and compassionate course.

Effectively excluding e-cigarettes from the market via stringent regulation would have the effect of killing smokers and protecting cigarette and pharmaceutical markets. E-cigarettes, a far safer form of nicotine delivery, should not be submitted to tougher regulation than cigarettes.

Americans should not have to die from misguided regulation.

"*The extent of this regulation needs to be carefully crafted, as the health impacts of e-cigarettes remain in scientific question.*"

It Is Too Early to Federally Regulate E-Cigarettes

Thomas A. Hemphill

Thomas A. Hemphill in an associate professor of strategy, innovation, and public policy at the University of Michigan-Flint's School of Management. In the following viewpoint, he opposes the federal regulation of electronic cigarettes, or e-cigarettes, without sound scientific evidence on its impacts. Considered as a tobacco product by the US Food and Drug Administration (FDA), the devices could be prematurely subjected to restrictions similar to that of conventional cigarettes, persists Hemphill, discouraging tobacco smokers from switching to this potentially less harmful alternative. Also, the author says that requiring warnings on e-cigarette packaging and limiting their marketing and availability of flavors at this time would be problematic.

Thomas A. Hemphill, "Electronic Cigarettes at a Regulatory Crossroads," *Regulation*, vol. 36, no. 3, Fall 2013, pp. 10–12. Copyright © 2013 Cato Institute. All rights reserved. Reproduced with permission.

As you read, consider the following questions:

1. What evidence does Hemphill provide that counters the FDA's findings that e-cigarettes contain tobacco-specific carcinogens?

2. How did e-cigarettes become regulated as tobacco products under the FDA, as told by Hemphill?

3. What are the regulatory policy options sought by state and local governments, as described by the author?

In 2000, a Chinese pharmacist named Hon Lik invented the modern electronic cigarette, or e-cigarette. The product uses a piezoelectric ultrasound-emitting element to vaporize a pressurized jet of liquid containing nicotine diluted in a propylene glycol solution. The "smoker" inhales the vapor through his mouth, simulating smoking. Though nicotine is addictive, e-cigarettes are thought to be much less of a health hazard than their combustible tobacco cousins, for both smoker and bystanders.

In 2011, retail e-cigarette sales in the United States reached $500 million, according to a recent *Wall Street Journal* article. Industry experts expect 2013 sales to reach $1 billion.

E-cigarettes are not without their critics, who see them as "gateway" products to eventual tobacco use and nicotine addiction. Many of the critics want e-cigarettes to be tightly regulated or removed from the marketplace altogether.

FDA Weighs In

In 2009, the U.S. Food and Drug Administration's Division of Pharmaceutical Analysis tested 19 varieties of e-cigarettes manufactured by two vendors, NJOY and Smoking Everywhere. The scientists found that tobacco-specific nitrosamines, known cancer-causing chemicals, were detected in all of the cartridges of one brand, and two of the cartridges from the other. In July of that year, the FDA announced that it would publicly discourage the use of e-cigarettes and raised concerns that they could be marketed to youth and that they did not have appropriate health warnings.

Critics of the FDA study responded that the detected harmful chemicals were measured by researchers at levels approximately one-millionth of the concentrations believed to be relevant to human health. Further, according to the results of a 2010 study by researchers at Boston University's School of Public Health, the levels of carcinogens in e-cigarettes are upwards of 1,000 times lower than tobacco cigarettes, had a level of toxicity similar to existing nicotine replacements (e.g., the nicotine patch, nicotine gum), and were found to be "much safer" than tobacco cigarettes.

Federal Control

Nonetheless, the federal government has attempted to tightly control access to e-cigarettes. On June 22, 2009, the Family Smoking Prevention and Tobacco Control Act was enacted into law. An amendment to the venerable [Federal] Food, Drug, and Cosmetic Act of 1938, the 2009 law gives the FDA authority to regulate products that are "made or derived from tobacco." E-cigarettes' nicotine is typically derived from the tobacco plant, so the legislation put the product under FDA authority.

Under the law, the FDA initially labeled some e-cigarettes as unapproved drug/medical device combination products, a designation that gave the agency considerable authority to control the product's availability. The FDA thus detained or refused to allow e-cigarettes to enter the United States.

One e-cigarette manufacturer, Sottera, challenged the FDA's action in court. In December of 2010, the U.S. Court of Appeals for the D.C. Circuit issued a 3–0 decision striking down the FDA's authority to regulate e-cigarettes as a drug/medical device. The U.S. Circuit Court subsequently held that e-cigarettes and other products made or derived from tobacco can be regulated by the FDA as "tobacco products," which limits the FDA's ability to suppress the devices. In January of 2011, the D.C. Appeals Court declined to review the circuit court's decision and the FDA decided not to appeal the decision further.

As a result of the *Sottera* [*Sottera v. Food & Drug Administration*] decision, in April 2011 the FDA announced that it planned to take the following steps to institute regulatory mechanisms for all "tobacco products" and all other products made or derived from tobacco:

- The FDA intends to propose a regulation that would extend the agency's "tobacco product" controls under Chapter IX of the [Federal] Food, Drug, and Cosmetic Act to other categories of tobacco products, as well as to the pre-market review requirements for "new tobacco products" and "modified-risk tobacco products."

- The FDA had previously issued draft guidance on products made or derived from tobacco regulated under the Tobacco Control Act (excluding those "marketed for therapeutic purposes"). The agency announced that it was considering whether to issue a guidance document and/or regulation on the "therapeutic" claims of e-cigarette manufacturers.

- The FDA intends to finalize already-issued draft guidance on prohibiting the marketing of "tobacco products" in combination with other FDA-regulated products.

- The FDA has already developed draft guidance explaining how manufacturers can request a determination from the agency that a "tobacco product" is "grandfathered" under Chapter IX requirements (i.e., marketed as of February 15, 2007), thus excluding the product from being subject to pre-market review as a "new tobacco product."

The FDA is moving its planned e-cigarette regulatory agenda forward. Last September [in 2012], the agency issued an advanced notice of rulemaking ("Non-Face-to-Face Sale and Distribution of Tobacco Products and Advertising, Promotion, and Marketing of Tobacco Products") on possible regulation. The comment period closed in December. As of this June, the FDA's rule ("Tobacco Products Subject to the Federal Food, Drug, and Cosmetic Act, as Amended by the Family Smoking Prevention and Tobacco Control Act") is in the "Proposed Rule Stage." In the above mentioned *Wall Street Journal* article, Mitch Zeller, director of the FDA's Center for Tobacco [Products], justified these steps by characterizing the present e-cigarette marketplace as the "wild, wild West" in terms of federal regulations.

Possible Regulation

E-cigarette regulatory policy options enacted by state and local governments generally consist of the following:

- Bans or restrictions on e-cigarette marketing to minors, or making unsubstantiated marketing claims

- Prohibiting e-cigarette smoking in public places

- Prohibiting e-cigarette sales to minors

At the state and local level, there appears to be little resistance to public policy restricting the sale or marketing of e-cigarettes to minors. Through 2012, 13 states had passed legislation prohibiting such sales. Several state and local governments have amended laws and ordinances against smoking in public places to include e-cigarettes, and that push is certain to continue.

Wrong Time for Federal Regulation?

The federal regulatory environment for e-cigarettes is evolving, but it has been bounded by *Sottera*: E-cigarettes are legally considered a "tobacco product." The FDA will thus likely attempt to regulate e-cigarettes in a fashion similar to tobacco cigarettes, and restrictions or bans will be initiated in the marketing and advertising of e-cigarettes. But the extent of this regulation needs to be carefully crafted, as the health impacts of e-cigarettes remain in scientific question. Beyond that, there is the question of what authority the FDA would have over e-cigarettes that do not derive their nicotine from tobacco— these products, after all, would not be "tobacco products."

Without a sound body of scientific knowledge to draw on, regulations requiring federal government warnings on e-cigarette packaging and restricting advertising and variety of flavors are problematic. In the aforementioned *Wall Street Journal* article, Richard Carmona, former U.S. surgeon general and a previous supporter of an outright ban on the consumer use of tobacco products, argues that it is important to explore alternatives to traditional cigarettes because "initial information certainly suggests there is significant potential for harm reduction" associated with e-cigarettes.

For those reasons, it is premature for the FDA to move forward with a regulatory agenda, if such regulatory policies discourage tobacco smokers from switching to potentially "less harmful to their health" e-cigarettes. In June, the Centers for Disease Control and Prevention reported that the percentage of U.S. adult smokers had declined to 18 percent in 2012, down from 20 percent in 2011 (and the previous seven years). A safer alternative to traditional tobacco-based products, if technologically feasible, should be encouraged by regulators for the benefit of those who choose to continue smoking and wish to reduce the adverse health effects from their use of tobacco.

| "*Experts say that [e-cigarettes] are probably safer, but safer doesn't mean safe.*"

It Is Too Early to Determine E-Cigarettes as a Safe Alternative to Smoking

Christopher Wanjek

In the following viewpoint, Christopher Wanjek claims that the safety of electronic cigarettes, or e-cigarettes, in comparison to traditional cigarettes is still under debate. While the devices may be safer, the author states, the delivery of nicotine to the lungs through e-cigarettes is similar to that of smoking, quickly creating a powerful addiction. Furthermore, he adds, nicotine is associated with cancer, birth defects, and developmental disorders. The possible negative effects of e-cigarettes are still unknown, and the conversion of tobacco smokers into "vapers" may not be a step toward a cleaner, healthier society, he proposes. Wanjek is the author of Food at Work *and* Bad Medicine, *as well as a columnist for LiveScience.*

As you read, consider the following questions:

1. In what way are e-cigarettes similar to cigarettes in the 1940s, in Wanjek's opinion?

Christopher Wanjek, "E-Cigarettes Just More Smoke and Mirrors, Doctors Say," Live-Science, November 21, 2013. www.livescience.com. Copyright © 2013 TechMedia Network. All rights reserved. Reproduced with permission.

2. According to Wanjek, how do nicotine patches and gum differ in the delivery of nicotine from e-cigarettes?

3. Why do e-cigarettes keep addicts in a "state of ambivalence," as expressed by Frank Leone?

A t first, electronic cigarettes were a novelty—something a braggart in a bar might puff to challenge the established no-smoking policy, marveling bystanders with the fact that the smoke released from the device was merely harmless vapor.

Now, e-cigarettes are poised to be a billion-dollar industry, claimed as the solution to bring in smokers from out of the cold, both figuratively and literally, as e-cigarettes promise to lift the stigma of smoking and are increasingly permitted at indoor facilities where smoking is banned.

So, are e-cigarettes safe? Well, they're not great for you, doctors say. What's being debated is the degree to which they are less dangerous than traditional cigarettes.

1940 Revisited

E-cigarettes are battery-powered devices, often shaped like traditional cigarettes, with a heating element that vaporizes a liquid nicotine solution, which must be replaced every few hundred puffs. Nicotine is inhaled into the lungs, and a largely odorless water vapor comes out of the device. Puffing an e-cigarette is called vaping.

Yet the industry's duplicity is clear to medical experts: E-cigarettes are marketed to smokers as a means to wean them off of tobacco (although studies show they don't help much); yet the same devices, some with fruity flavors, are marketed to young people who don't smoke, which could get them hooked.

Hooked? Yes, e-cigarettes are a nicotine-delivery system, highly addictive and ultimately harmful because of their nicotine.

Cancer and respiratory experts see the same ploy being played out today with e-cigarettes as was done in the 1940s with cigarettes, when America started smoking en masse. They often are distributed for free and pitched by celebrities and even doctors as cool, liberating and safe.

In an ad for a product called blu eCigs, celebrity Jenny McCarthy, infamous for encouraging parents not to vaccinate their children, encourages young adults to vape, enlisting words such as "freedom" and the promise of sex. In another ad, for V2 Cigs, a medical doctor named Matthew Huebner—who is presented without affiliation but is associated with a Cleveland Clinic facility in Weston, Fla.—implies that vaping is as harmless as boiling water.

As for the notion of e-cigs as liberating, the cost of a year's worth of e-cigarette nicotine cartridges is about $600, compared with $1,000 yearly for a half-pack a day of regular cigarettes.

As for whether they're safe, it's a matter of comparing the advantages of one addiction over another.

E-Cigarettes Not a Patch

One would think that vaping has to be safer than smoking real cigarettes. Experts say they are probably safer, but safer doesn't mean safe.

"Cigarettes have their risk profile," said Dr. Frank Leone, a pulmonary expert at the University of Pennsylvania medical center in Philadelphia. And just about everyone who breathes understands the risks: circulatory disease and myriad cancers, for starters. "E-cigarettes might be better off compared to that profile. But that doesn't mean they don't have their own risk profile."

A top concern is the nicotine delivery rate, Leone said. With nicotine patches and gum, the nicotine delivery is regulated, with small amounts of nicotine released slowly into the bloodstream. But with traditional cigarettes and now e-cigarettes, heat creates a freebase form of nicotine that is

The Unknowns of Inhaling Nicotine Vapor

The short- and long-term effects of inhaling nicotine vapor are unknown, and there are no health warnings that appear on the e-cigarette packaging. In an article published in 2010 in *Nicotine & Tobacco Research*, the authors reported that e-cigarettes require stronger suction (inhalation) than conventional cigarettes and that this could have a detrimental effect on the health of the smoker. In addition, they noted that since the vapor inhaled with each breath decreases during smoking, not only does this require increasing the puff strength, but it also varies the amount of nicotine inhaled with each puff, making the uniform dosing of nicotine unreliable.

Medifocus Guidebook on Smoking Cessation.
Silver Spring, MD: Medifocus.com Inc., 2011, p. 26.

more addictive—or what smokers would call more satisfying. The nicotine goes right into the lungs, where it is quickly channeled into the heart and then pumped into the brain.

Once addicted, the body will crave nicotine. And although nicotine isn't the most dangerous toxin in tobacco's arsenal, this chemical nevertheless is a cancer-promoting agent, and is associated with birth defects and developmental disorders.

A study published in 2006 in the journal *Obstetrics & Gynecology*, for example, found that women who chewed nicotine gum during pregnancy had a higher risk of birth defects compared to other nonsmokers.

Great Unknowns

This great unknown of possible negative health effects, along with the lack of regulation of e-cigarettes, scares experts like

Leone. The products come bereft of health warnings. How many pregnant women will vape following McCarthy's promotion?

As for their merits in smoking cessation, e-cigarettes don't appear very helpful. A study published last month [October 2013] in the journal *Addictive Behaviors* found that most smokers who used them while they tried to quit either became hooked on vaping, or reverted back to smoking cigarettes. A study published Nov. 16 in the journal the *Lancet* found no statistically significant difference in the merits of the e-cigarette over the nicotine patch in terms of helping people quit.

Leone said that e-cigarettes might not help people quit smoking because the device keeps addicts in a state of ambivalence—the illusion of doing something positive to mitigate the guilt that comes from smoking, but all the while maintaining the ritual of smoking.

The Jenny McCarthy blu eCigs ad hints at this notion, with such phrases as "smarter alternative to cigarettes," "without the guilt" and "now that I switched . . . I feel better about myself."

Editors of the *Lancet* called promotion of e-cigarettes "a moral quandary" because of this potential to replace harmful cigarettes with something slightly less harmful yet just as addictive. Other researchers agree that e-cigarettes might help some people quit, but at a population level, converting millions of smokers into vapers still addicted to nicotine might not lead to the cleaner, greener, healthier world implied by e-cigarette manufacturers.

And then there's the issue of not knowing what's in the e-cigarette nicotine cartridge.

"It's an amazing thing to watch a new product like that just kind of appear; there's no quality control," said Dr. Richard Hurt, director of the Mayo Clinic's Nicotine Dependence

Center in Rochester, Minn. "Many of them are manufactured in China under no control conditions, so the story is yet to be completely told."

The authors of the *Lancet* study, all based in New Zealand, called for countries to regulate the manufacturing and sale of e-cigarettes. The U.S. Food and Drug Administration, which does not approve any e-cigarettes for therapeutic purpose, said it plans to propose a regulation to extend the definition of "tobacco product" under the [Family Smoking Prevention and] Tobacco Control Act to gain more authority to regulate products such as e-cigarettes.

| "In reality, switching from cigarettes to [smokeless tobacco] will dramatically reduce your oral cancer risk (and your risk of lung disease, heart disease, and many other diseases)."

Smokeless Tobacco Is a Safer Alternative to Smoking

Carl V. Phillips

Carl V. Phillips is the director and chief scientist at Tobacco harmreduction.org. In the following viewpoint, Phillips asserts that using smokeless tobacco is much safer than smoking. Unlike cigarettes, the total risk of oral cancer from smokeless tobacco is very small, he states. Even if smokeless tobacco multiplied the risk by four times, Phillips explains, the risk would still be very low—especially compared with the risk of dying from smoking-related lung and heart diseases. Furthermore, research on smokeless tobacco as a cause of cardiovascular disease has found no increased risk, Phillips continues. It is widely viewed as "not a safe alternative to smoking" he contends, because required labels on packaging are misinterpreted.

As you read, consider the following questions:

1. How does Phillips support his stance that the risk of heart disease or stroke from using smokeless tobacco is very low?

2. What is the real meaning of "not safe" in describing smokeless tobacco as a smoking alternative, according to the author?

3. How does Phillips address the assertion that smokeless tobacco contains potentially harmful chemicals?

Contrary to popular belief, smokeless tobacco is not a major health hazard. In fact, it has not been definitively linked to any deadly disease. More important, to the extent that it causes any risks, the scientific evidence clearly shows that the risks are very small.

This might surprise you. We will admit that it surprised every one of us when we first learned it. Because there is so much misinformation about ST [smokeless tobacco], much of it spread by otherwise legitimate health authorities, it can be difficult to find the truth. Below, we take up the question of how to sort out truth, lies, and genuine scientific uncertainty. Here, we present what the scientific evidence actually shows.

Doesn't Smokeless Tobacco Cause Oral Cancer (Cancer of the Mouth)? If So, Very Rarely.

There is overwhelming evidence that any risk for oral cancer (cancer of the mouth) from ST is very low.

This is an important question in the ST debate, so here is a little background first. Oral cancer (cancer of the mouth and surrounding areas) is a fairly rare disease in Western countries, and in most cases is caused by smoking. Smoking can increase your risk of oral cancer by eight or ten times, much more than even the worst-case-scenario estimate for ST.

The American government attributes about 75% of all oral cancer deaths in that country to smoking combined with drinking. In other words, the best thing you can do to reduce the risk for oral cancer is not to smoke.

Even if ST did cause a measurable increase in oral cancer risk, the total risk would still be small. The "baseline" risk for oral cancer (the risk for people who do not smoke or drink a lot of alcohol) is quite low. So even if ST multiplied that risk by 2 or even 4, the total risk of dying from it would still be very small compared to the risks of the lung and heart diseases caused by smoking. (Consider if you had a choice between doubling your chances of dying by getting hit by lightning versus doubling your chances of dying in a car crash. Doubling your risk from lightning would hardly matter because it is so rare in the first place; two times a very small number is still a very small number. But doubling your risk from a car crash would be a lot more worrisome.)

In one of the most remarkable marketing successes ever, anti-ST activists have convinced people that, "if I switch from smoking to dipping, I will just trade lung cancer for mouth cancer." In reality, switching from cigarettes to ST will dramatically reduce your oral cancer risk (and your risk of lung disease, heart disease, and many other diseases), and even if that were not true, the trade-off would still be a good one because the risk of oral cancer for nonsmokers is so low in the first place.

Having said all that, what is the answer to the original question? What does the scientific evidence say about the risk for oral cancer from smokeless tobacco?

It turns out that the evidence clearly shows there is very little risk. When looking at scientific research, it is necessary to look at all of it, not just one or two particular studies. As with most things we study in health science, the results vary. A few studies find that people who use ST have a higher risk for oral cancer but most studies have found that the risk is very low. Some even show a negative association. This is the same to say, if someone just picked out those studies and ignored the rest, they might conclude that using ST protects you against getting oral cancer. Of course, picking just a few studies with extreme results is just bad science.

When we look at all the scientific evidence, it averages out to there being either no risk or very little risk (it is impossible to tell the difference between those two conclusions because health science methods are always imperfect). By "very little," we mean that using smokeless tobacco might cause a 10% or 20% increase in the risk for oral cancer compared to not smoking or not drinking heavily. The evidence shows it is extremely unlikely that the increase in risk is as high as 50% (which is still much less than the risk from smoking).

If you do not want to delve into the technical details, the previous points and our calculation of the comparative risk of smoking and smokeless tobacco are all you need to know. . . .

Oral leukoplakia occurs commonly in ST users, but it primarily represents irritation and only very rarely progresses to oral cancer.

Does Smokeless Tobacco Cause Other Cancers? If So, Very Rarely.

Again, the answer has to be that there is no conclusive evidence that it does, but it is certainly possible that it does at some very low level. There is no clear evidence that ST causes any cancer. Hence, the evidence indicates that if there is any risk, it is small.

Other than oral cancer, the cancers that seem most likely to be associated with ST are laryngeal, esophageal (throat), and gastric (stomach), since those are the other parts of the body that come in contact with the tobacco. For these sites, along with a few others, there is plenty of scientific evidence that there is no substantially elevated risk. As with oral cancer, researchers have looked for an association and have failed to find one. For other cancer sites there are few or no studies, so we do not have any evidence one way or the other. However, studies that look at all cancers combined have failed to find an increase among smokeless tobacco users, so there cannot be a very big increase for any particular cancer.

Does Smokeless Tobacco Cause Heart Disease or Stroke? The Risk Is Probably Quite Small.

There may be some small risk, though there is no definitive evidence. Most studies of cardiovascular disease and smokeless tobacco have found no increased risk. However, because nicotine is a mild stimulant, it might increase the risk of certain cardiovascular outcomes, such as stroke. Many stimulants have been linked to some risk for fatal cardiovascular events. This does not prove that nicotine causes such risk, but it suggests that it is plausible.

The available evidence shows that if there is any risk from smokeless tobacco, it is low, less than a 20% increase (for comparison, smoking is estimated to roughly double this risk, a 100% increase). This is potentially more important than a similar percentage increase in oral cancer risk, since cardiovascular disease is a lot more common. If the risk of cardiovascular disease increases by as much as 20% then smokeless tobacco might cause 3% or 4% of the risk associated with smoking. That is still a lot better than smoking, of course, but worse than 1%. Fortunately, most of the evidence suggests that nicotine without the smoke is not actually quite that bad. But it would be useful to do more research to find out more. Unlike with oral cancer, there is not enough available research about cardiovascular disease for us to feel entirely comfortable in our conclusions.

What Does This All Mean for the Total Risk Compared to Smoking? Using Smokeless Tobacco Is Much Safer than Smoking.

It means that the risk is tiny compared to smoking. You might hear other estimates but as far as we know, we are the only ones who have actually done the calculation. Our calculations show that if we take a worst-case scenario and assess the risks for cancer and cardiovascular disease, the total risk from ST is only a few percent of that from smoking.

Due to the limitations of health science, we cannot be sure exactly how the risks compare. But we can be very sure that the total risk of dying from ST use is less than 1% of that from smoking. That is, for any plausible levels of risk for disease from ST, any values that are not clearly ruled out by the science, the total risk is less than 1/100th that from smoking. There is no legitimate scientific doubt that someone's risk drops by at least 99% by using ST instead of smoking.

So Why Do So Many People Say "Smokeless Tobacco Is Not a Safe Alternative to Cigarettes"?

The main reason that this phrase is so common is that the U.S. and Canadian governments require a version of it to be printed on packages of ST products. This is unfortunate, since most people interpret the phrase "not safe" to mean "dangerous." The phrase "not a safe alternative to cigarettes" is understood as "just as bad as cigarettes."

Strictly speaking, the statement is true. If we interpret "safe" to mean "100% safe; creating no health risk at all" then smokeless tobacco is not "safe" (and neither is anything else. Chances are that somewhere, sometime, somehow, broccoli has killed someone). Smokeless tobacco may not be a "safe" alternative, but neither are any of the other products used to help people stop smoking. Certainly trying to quit and failing, or smoking for another year or two before quitting, are not "safe" either. ST is much safer, however, and that is what matters.

Think about this: Driving safely and properly is not a safe alternative to speeding while drunk and not wearing a seat belt. But it is very close. It might even reduce the risk by as much as 95%. Somehow, there seems to be no confusion about which of those options we think someone should choose. There should be no confusion about tobacco products either. Smokeless tobacco is much less harmful, and the fact that it is not 100% safe does not change this.

Are You Saying That Smokeless Tobacco Is Harmless? No.

As far as we know, no one is saying that. As we noted, it is possible that smokeless tobacco causes cancer or other deadly diseases at some very low level. We know that the nicotine has short-term cardiovascular effects which may be a little bit harmful. Nothing is 100% harmless, and this includes smokeless tobacco. This does not change the fact that it is a much less harmful alternative to smoking.

What About All the Chemicals in Smokeless Tobacco That I Hear About?

Sometimes people who are opposed to harm reduction or any use of ST present a list of potentially harmful constituents. What they do not tell you is that many of those chemicals are in other plants, including the healthy vegetables that you eat. A little bit of all the metals on Earth, including cadmium, polonium, and others that are quite bad for you in large quantities, end up in everything. They are in tobacco, carrots, wheat, and even the water you drink. There are also organic molecules like formaldehyde in most every life-form on Earth, including tobacco. Again, concentrated in large quantities, you would certainly want to stay away from some of these chemicals, but the amount that naturally occurs in plants (and in your own body) is not a problem. We are lucky that there are not a lot of anti-broccoli advocates out there trying to trick you into not eating it because it contains some cadmium.

One set of chemicals that are talked about a lot in the science are nitrosamines, or tobacco-specific nitrosamines (TSNAs). Nitrosamines are a class of chemicals that we are exposed to in food and through other pathways. Some of these are known to be carcinogens in some quantities. Whether the TSNAs might be carcinogens is the subject of debate. Fortunately, it does not matter whether these chemicals might cause cancer since we have evidence about whether ST itself causes cancer. The evidence shows that people who use ST do not have measurable increases in cancer rates or mortality. So it does not really matter what chemicals are there.

Think about this: If you met a thin person who always ate huge amounts of food, would you tell him that eating all that food is making him overweight? Obviously not, since you can directly observe that he is not overweight. All this talk about chemicals is like that. If all you knew about a person was that he always overeats, it might suggest that he would be overweight. Similarly, if you only knew about the chemicals and had never observed the actual health effect of the products, the chemical analysis could suggest that there might be a health effect. But once you observe that someone is thin (or observe that smokeless tobacco users do not have elevated disease rates), the suggestive evidence is no longer informative. It can only be used to trick you into thinking there is a health effect when the evidence actually says otherwise.

| "It is a known cause of human cancer,
as it increases the risk of developing
cancer of the oral cavity."

Smokeless Tobacco Should Be Included in Smoking Bans

Centers for Disease Control and Prevention

In the following viewpoint, the Centers for Disease Control and Prevention (CDC) encourages applying smoking bans to smokeless tobacco products. The CDC asserts that these products—which contain more than twenty-eight cancer-causing agents—are not safer than cigarettes and, in many cases, lead to cigarette smoking. The CDC outlines which groups are at the highest risk for developing tobacco-related cancer and other health concerns such as leukoplakia. The CDC is the nation's health protection agency; it works to save lives and protect people from health threats at home and abroad.

As you read, consider the following questions:

1. According to the CDC, how many cancer-causing agents does smokeless tobacco contain?

2. What does the CDC identify as the two main types of smokeless tobacco in the United States?

Centers for Disease Control and Prevention, "Smokeless Tobacco (Dip, Chew, Snuff)," www.cdc.gov, February 23, 2011.

3. According to the viewpoint, smokeless tobacco use is highest among which groups of people?

Smokeless tobacco is a significant health risk and is not a safe substitute for smoking cigarettes. Smokeless tobacco contains 28 cancer-causing agents (carcinogens). Smokeless tobacco use can lead to nicotine addiction and dependence. Adolescents who use smokeless tobacco are more likely to become cigarette smokers.

The two main types of smokeless tobacco in the United States are chewing tobacco and snuff. Chewing tobacco comes in the form of loose leaf, plug, or twist. Snuff is finely ground tobacco that can be dry, moist, or in sachets (tea bag–like pouches). Although some forms of snuff can be used by sniffing or inhaling into the nose, most smokeless tobacco users place the product in their cheek or between their gum and cheek. Users then suck on the tobacco and spit out the tobacco juices, which is why smokeless tobacco is often referred to as spit or spitting tobacco.

It is a known cause of human cancer, as it increases the risk of developing cancer of the oral cavity.

Who's at Risk?

- Smokeless tobacco use in the United States is higher among young white males; American Indians/Alaska Natives; people living in southern and north-central states; and people who are employed in blue-collar occupations, service/laborer jobs, or who are unemployed.

- Nationally, an estimated 3 percent of adults are current smokeless tobacco users. Smokeless tobacco use is much higher among men (6 percent) than women (less than 1 percent).

- In the United States, 9 percent of American Indian/ Alaska Natives, 4 percent of whites, 2 percent of African

Americans, 1 percent of Hispanics, and less than 1 percent of Asian American adults are current smokeless tobacco users.

- An estimated 8 percent of high school students are current smokeless tobacco users. Smokeless tobacco is more common among males (13.6 percent) than female high school students (2.2 percent). Estimates by race/ethnicity are 10.2 percent for white, 5.1 percent for Hispanic, and 1.7 percent for African American high school students.

- An estimated 3 percent of middle school students are current smokeless tobacco users. Smokeless tobacco is more common among male (4 percent) than female (2 percent) middle school students. Estimates by race/ethnicity are 3 percent for white, 1 percent for Asian, 2 percent for African American, and 4 percent for Hispanic middle school students.

Can It Be Prevented?

Yes. Hopefully by clarifying that smokeless tobacco is not safe, we can help people make an informed decision about its use. School-based programs are an opportunity to discourage youth on the use of smokeless tobacco. The film industry can also influence the public by not glamorizing any form of tobacco use. More community-wide efforts aimed at prevention and cessation of smokeless tobacco use among young people are needed. In addition, opportunities for intervention occur in all clinical settings and require knowledgeable and committed health care professionals. Training programs for health care providers should include components to help make smokeless tobacco counseling a higher priority.

Case Example

Jimmy is a good-looking kid and friends with just about everyone. Recently some of his friends have started using smokeless tobacco. He used to think it was something the old folks used to do with spit coming out of their mouths. He'll never admit it, but the sight of the spitting used to make him want to puke. The stuff smelled awful and looked grotesque.

However, the stuff his friends use doesn't seem to be like that. What they use smells like apple and cherry with just a little bit of the awful stuff mixed in. They just put it in their mouths and suck. They don't even have to spit. Some of the older kids have been using these products for a few years now.

Recently, he noticed some of those kids had white areas in their mouths. He asked them what it was, and they told him that the doctor had said it was "leukoplakia, whatever that was." He also noticed that his friends' gums were going back, like old folks.

In addition to being good-looking and friendly, Jimmy was also smart. He went online to find out more about leukoplakia. He learned that it can be caused by cigarette smoking or chewing tobacco, and it can lead to cancer. He also found that smokeless tobacco made the gums go back, which explained the "old folks' gums" on his friends.

He decided not to take the smokeless tobacco when offered. He told his friends about what he had learned and asked the school newspaper to publish an article about the health hazards of smokeless tobacco. He petitioned the student council to ban ALL smokeless tobacco on campus. This was so successful that using chewing tobacco became an "uncool" behavior everywhere on campus.

Periodical and Internet Sources Bibliography

The following articles have been selected to supplement the diverse views presented in this chapter.

Ethan Epstein	"Thank You for Not Vaping: The Irrational Hostility to E-Cigarettes," *Weekly Standard*, August 5, 2013.
Anne Harding	"Most Youth Who Use Smokeless Tobacco Are Smokers, Too," Reuters, August 8, 2013.
Steven Ross Johnson	"Sparking Controversy: Rise in E-Cigarette Use Has Public Health Experts Questioning Their Safety, Effectiveness as Harm-Reduction Device," *Modern Healthcare*, September 23, 2013.
Lynn Love	"A Smarter Nicotine Fix? The Truth Behind E-Cigarettes," *Dance Magazine*, February 2014.
Ruth Macklin	"E-Cigarettes: Is Liquid Nicotine Safe?," *Huffington Post*, June 4, 2014.
Michael McCord	"Are Regulations Necessary for E-Cigarettes?," *New Hampshire Business Review*, March 7, 2014.
Liz Neporent	"E-Cigarette Debate Reignites with New Vaping Report," ABC News, September 6, 2014.
Alessandra Potenza	"Smoke Signals: Why Electronic Cigarettes— Unregulated and Increasingly Popular Among Young People—Are Worrying Some U.S. Officials," *New York Times Upfront*, December 9, 2013.
Andrew Stuttaford	"Vaper Strain: The Senseless Demonization of E-Cigarettes," *National Review Online*, September 2, 2013.
Emily Thomas	"Liquid Nicotine in E-Cigarettes Could Be Deadly," *Huffington Post*, March 24, 2014.

CHAPTER 4

How Do Media Impact the Choice to Smoke or Not Smoke?

Chapter Preface

While the popularity of social media and mobile technology is exploding among children and adolescents, the Internet as an influence on youth tobacco use has yet to be scrutinized like traditional cigarette advertising or smoking in movies. "Although numerous studies have examined Internet use patterns for various purposes, the effect of Internet use on teen smoking initiation has received little attention in studies," state Susan R. Forsyth, Christine Kennedy, and Ruth E. Malone of the Department of Social and Behavioral Sciences, School of Nursing at the University of California, San Francisco. They explain that advertising and promotional spending includes "Web-based activities, 'viral' marketing, and insertion of their products into popular culture."

Citing one of the first studies on the topic, Forsyth, Kennedy, and Malone maintain that smoking imagery online and its effects on youths should be a concern, as it adopts the strategies of conventional tobacco advertisements. "Like other, more traditional pro-smoking imagery, many of these Web sites portrayed smokers as young, thin, and attractive, leading exciting lives," they state. Also, Forsyth, Kennedy, and Malone advise that such content may have adult themes. "The sites also were found to be accessible to children, and they often mentioned brands or featured brand images and displayed pictures depicting smoking, usually with female smokers. Several displayed partial or full nudity, linking sex with cigarette use."

Furthermore, Forsyth, Kennedy, and Malone contend that tobacco companies' home pages are viewed mostly by adults, but the nature of the Internet can enable them to reach younger audiences in less visible ways. "Although all tobacco companies had formal Web sites, they are not likely destinations for the average browsing teen, who spends the majority of his or her screen time on social networking sites. However, given the vastness and relatively anonymous nature of the Internet," they explain, "it is likely that plenty of opportunity exists for the tobacco industry to insert pro-tobacco imagery in other, less formal venues." In the following chapter, the authors debate media's power over shaping the choice to use tobacco.

> "Advertising and promotional activities by tobacco companies have been shown to cause the onset and continuation of smoking among adolescents and young adults."

Tobacco Marketing Influences Youth Smoking

Center for Public Health and Tobacco Policy

The Center for Public Health and Tobacco Policy is a project of the Center for Law and Social Responsibility, providing support and resources to tobacco control communities in New York and Vermont. In the following viewpoint, it contends that strong evidence shows that tobacco marketing influences youth smoking and that tobacco products are intentionally advertised and promoted to teens. The scientific data, the center claims, indicates that cigarette advertisements routinely reach teens, are perceived as appealing by teens, and increase teen urges to smoke. Additionally, numerous studies demonstrate that point-of-sale marketing is associated with youth smoking initiation and prevalence, argues the center.

"Section III. The Effect: Tobacco Marketing Increases Youth Tobacco Use," *Cause and Effect: Tobacco Marketing Increases Youth Tobacco Use*, Findings of the 2012 Surgeon General's Report, May 2012.

As you read, consider the following questions:

1. What adolescent behaviors are influenced by tobacco marketing, according to the center?

2. Why is point-of-sale marketing an important channel for tobacco companies, as stated by the center?

3. As described by the center, how effective is brand imagery on cigarette packaging?

Since the 1994 surgeon general's report, considerable evidence has accumulated that supports a causal association between marketing efforts of tobacco companies and the initiation and progression of tobacco use among young people. . . . This body of evidence consistently and coherently points to the intentional marketing of tobacco products to youth as being a cause of young people's tobacco use.

Advertising and promotional activities by tobacco companies have been shown to cause the onset and continuation of smoking among adolescents and young adults.

[P]romotion and advertising by the tobacco industry *cause* tobacco use, including its initiation among youth. This conclusion has been buttressed by a multitude of scientific and governmental reports, and the strength of the evidence for causality continues to grow.

A 2003 systematic review of the published longitudinal studies on the impact of advertising concluded "that tobacco advertising and promotion increases the likelihood that adolescents will start to smoke." Both the industry's own internal documents and its testimony in court proceedings, as well as widely accepted principles of advertising and marketing, also support the conclusion that tobacco advertising recruits new users during their youth.

There is strong empirical evidence that tobacco companies' advertising and promotions affect awareness of smoking and of particular brands, the recognition and recall of cigarette advertising, attitudes about smoking, intentions to smoke, and actual smoking behavior. In fact, children appear to be even more responsive to advertising appeals than are adults.

In addition, industry marketing efforts directed at young adults, which are permitted under the [Master Settlement Agreement], have indirect spillover effects on youth through young adults who are aspirational role models for youth.

There is extensive scientific data showing (1) adolescents are regularly exposed to cigarette advertising, (2) they find many of these advertisements appealing, (3) advertisements tend to make smoking appealing, and (4) advertisements serve to increase adolescents' desire to smoke.

There is strong and consistent evidence that marketing influences adolescent smoking behavior, including selection of brands, initiation of smoking, and overall consumption of cigarettes.

[Research] findings suggest that after the Master Settlement Agreement, cigarette advertising continues to reach adolescents, that adolescents continue to be responsive to cigarette advertising, and that those who are responsive are more likely to initiate smoking.

NCI's [National Cancer Institute's] tobacco control monograph, "The Role of the Media in Promoting and Reducing Tobacco Use" (NCI 2008), also examined the evidence on how tobacco marketing efforts affect tobacco use among adolescents. Using numerous studies and tobacco industry documents, the report concluded that even brief exposure to tobacco advertising influences attitudes and perceptions about smoking and adolescents' intentions to smoke. In addition, the evidence showed that exposure to cigarette advertising influences nonsmoking adolescents to begin smoking and move toward regular smoking.

The continuously accumulating evidence from the studies that have addressed the effect of advertising on smoking is consistent with a dose-dependent causal relationship.

Taking together the epidemiology of adolescent tobacco use, internal tobacco company documents describing the importance of new smokers, analysis of the design of marketing campaigns, the actual imagery communicated in the $10-billion-a-year marketing effort, the conclusions of official government reports, and the weight of the scientific evidence, it is concluded that advertising and promotion have caused youth to start smoking and continue to smoke.

[D]espite claims from cigarette manufacturers that marketing and promotion of their products are intended to increase market share and promote brand loyalty among adult consumers, the evidence presented in this [viewpoint] is sufficient to conclude that marketing efforts and promotion by tobacco companies show a consistent dose-response relationship in the initiation and progression of tobacco use among young people.

Point-of-Sale Marketing Increases Youth Tobacco Use

[A] longitudinal study of more than 1,600 adolescents aged 11–14 years found that the odds of initiating smoking more than doubled for adolescents reporting that they visited the types of stores that contain the most cigarette advertising (convenience stores, liquor stores, and small grocery stores) two or more times a week. [The study controlled for] risk factors typically associated with uptake of smoking such as smoking by family and friends.

A systematic review of eight cross-sectional studies on the impact of tobacco promotion at the point of sale consistently found significant associations between exposure to point-of-sale tobacco promotions and initiation of smoking or susceptibility to that behavior. In conclusion, tobacco marketing at the point of sale is associated with the use of tobacco by youth. Because point-of-sale marketing is an important channel for the tobacco companies, with very few restrictions, con-

Tobacco Advertising Budgets Are Unjustified

Tobacco companies claim that advertising is aimed at developing brand loyalty and attracting 'switchers' and not at targeting youth. Yet relatively few smokers switch brands—it has been estimated at around 9 per cent. This would not justify the large advertising budgets. Advertising budgets for tobacco are disproportionately high compared to other consumer products. In the US in 1999, $8.24 billion was spent on tobacco advertising, an increase of 22 per cent over 1998, and a sixfold increase over 1963, after adjusting for inflation.

Geraint Howells, The Tobacco Challenge: Legal Policy and Consumer Protection. *Burlington, VT: Ashgate Publishing Company, 2011.*

sumers, including children, are unavoidably exposed to pro-smoking messages when they shop or when they are simply passing by stores.

Location of Retail Stores

Neighborhoods that are more densely populated with stores selling tobacco may promote adolescent smoking not only by increasing access but also by increasing environmental cues to smoke.

In Chicago, Illinois, youth in areas with the highest density of retail tobacco outlets were 13% more likely to have smoked in the past month than those living in areas with the lowest density of outlets. In a California study, the prevalence of current smoking was higher in high schools with the highest density of tobacco outlets in their neighborhoods than in high schools in neighborhoods without any outlets; the density of retail cigarette advertising in school neighborhoods was also associated with smoking prevalence.

The presence of heavy cigarette advertising in [convenience] stores has been shown to increase the likelihood of exposing youth to pro-smoking messages, which can increase initiation rates among those exposed, particularly if stores are near schools.

[R]esearch on the location of retail outlets selling cigarettes indicated that experimental smoking among youth was related to the density of tobacco outlets both in high school neighborhoods and in neighborhoods where youth live.

Tobacco Product Displays and Packaging

The brand imagery on cigarette packages is effective to the point that large majorities of youth—including nonsmoking youth—demonstrate high levels of recall for leading package designs.

Two studies conducted in countries that ban cigarette advertising at the point of sale confirm that exposure of adolescents to pack displays is associated with increased intentions to smoke among youth.

[I]n two experimental studies, students who saw photos of stores with tobacco displays and advertising were more likely to overestimate the percentage of adolescents and adults who smoke and to believe that tobacco is easier to buy than were those who saw photos without retail tobacco materials.

Recent research suggests that even when terms such as "light" and "mild" are prohibited in tobacco packaging and advertising, a significant proportion of adult and youth smokers continue to report false beliefs about the relative risk of cigarette brands. Studies suggest that the use of lighter colors on cigarette packs to imply lightness, as well as replacement words such as "smooth," have the same misleading effect as "light" and "mild" labels.

Price Promotions That Reduce the Cost of Tobacco Products

[Y]outh respond more than adults to price changes in terms of their use of tobacco.

Given the greater price sensitivity of smoking among young people . . . the industry's targeted pricing and price-reducing promotion strategies will have their greatest impact on youth and young adults.

[A] growing and increasingly sophisticated body of research has clearly demonstrated that tobacco use among young people is responsive to changes in the prices of tobacco products. Most of these studies have found that usage levels among young people change more in response to price changes than do usage levels among adults. This research includes studies that have looked at the consumption of cigarettes and smokeless tobacco products as well as various stages of cigarette smoking among youth and young adults.

In considering the numerous studies demonstrating that tobacco use among young people is responsive to changes in the prices of tobacco products, it can be concluded that the industry's extensive use of price-reducing promotions has led to higher rates of tobacco use among young people than would have occurred in the absence of these promotions.

| "Large independent studies have failed to find a statistically significant connection between tobacco advertising, consumption, and youth smoking."

Tobacco Marketing Does Not Influence Youth Smoking

Patrick Basham

In the following viewpoint, Patrick Basham maintains that research has not found a significant link between advertising and smoking rates among young people. Moreover, the author continues, youth smoking is not impacted by pricing because young people obtain cigarettes from family and friends, and the majority of smokers between twelve and eighteen consume the three costliest brands. Therefore, he accuses the government of basing tobacco policy on its own faulty evidence. Basham is the director of the Democracy Institute and an adjunct scholar at the Cato Institute. He is the author of Butt Out!: How Philip Morris Burned Ted Kennedy, the FDA & the Anti-Tobacco Movement *and coauthor of* The Plain Truth: Does Packaging Influence Smoking?

As you read, consider the following questions:

1. What evidence does Basham say reinforces the fact that tobacco advertising does not influence youth smoking?

2. Why is evidence supporting Canada's bans on tobacco displays untrue, in Basham's words?

3. What do tax increases for tobacco succeed in, as purported by Basham?

Tobacco policy currently rests on two claims: tobacco advertising and promotion are the major reasons why young people begin to smoke; and young people are particularly sensitive to the price of cigarettes. From these two claims follow the central elements of tobacco policy, namely that all forms of tobacco advertising and promotion, including tobacco displays, should be banned, and tobacco should be heavily taxed in order to prevent or at least reduce underage tobacco use.

Unfortunately, neither of these claims nor policies meets the standards of evidence-based policy making. Both are, instead, products of advocacy-based 'research' carried out by anti-tobacco lobby groups.

In evidence-based policy making, as in evidence-based clinical medicine, practices and decisions are based on rigorous, systematic reviews of 'best practice', that is, therapies and interventions that work the best in reducing morbidity and mortality. Evidence, and evidence alone, not theory or tradition, drives practice.

Tobacco Advertising's Impact Is Mixed

The empirical record about tobacco advertising's effect on young people is decidedly mixed. Large independent studies have failed to find a statistically significant connection between tobacco advertising, consumption, and youth smoking. Indeed, the two major UK government-commissioned studies on tobacco advertising and marketing failed to find a causal link between advertising and young people starting to smoke.

This lack of evidence is confirmed by the fact that countries that have had advertising bans for a quarter century or more have not experienced statistically significant declines in youth smoking. Consumption and prevalence data from 145 countries find little evidence that the entire range of tobacco control measures, including advertising restrictions and bans, has a statistically significant effect on smoking prevalence in *any* country.

Yet, the government pushes ahead with increasingly draconian restrictions on tobacco advertising through legislation to ban the display of all tobacco products. Even though the Department of Health [DoH] claims that there is substantial evidence to show that such bans will reduce youth smoking, this is not the case.

The evidence in support of tobacco display bans, just as for tobacco advertising bans, is embarrassingly thin. Most studies show that tobacco displays have no statistically significant effect on youth smoking.

The most frequently quoted studies actually found that seeing tobacco displays had no effect on youth intentions to smoke. None of the so-called evidence about tobacco displays provides compelling behavioural evidence that any young person started smoking after seeing tobacco displays.

The evidence from the experience of other countries that have tried display bans does not support the claim that they reduce youth smoking. The government has repeatedly claimed that Canada, where several provinces have banned tobacco displays, shows that such bans result in fewer tobacco sales and fewer youth smoking.

The government knew that this claim, and the evidence that it was based on, was not true. Recently released DoH correspondence shows that the government was told in a March 2009 email that removing tobacco displays in Canada 'has not caused a decline in tobacco sales or discourage[ed] kids from smoking'.

Yet, the anti-tobacco lobby continues to push for even more far-reaching tobacco control legislation. This past week [in September 2009], Action on Smoking and Health (Ash) trumpeted a new study about the influence of tobacco packages as proof that putting all tobacco products in plain packages was now required. Ash's Deborah Arnott told the BBC that: "This research shows that the only way of putting an end to this misleading marketing is to require all tobacco products to be sold in plain packaging."

What Arnott did not tell the BBC was that she and Martin Dockrell, Ash's campaign manager, were not only two of the authors of the very study they so fulsomely praised, but Ash, along with the DoH, paid for the study.

Considerable previous research has shown that plain packaging of cigarettes will do nothing to reduce youth smoking. A study from Canada's York University, which asked young people about what effect plain packaging would have on their smoking decisions, found that 90 percent of daily smokers said they would smoke more or the same if cigarettes were in plain packages.

Less Sensitive to Price Increases

What then of high taxes to discourage or prevent youth smoking?

The claim that high tobacco taxes will reduce smoking is an odd one since we have been taught that smoking is addictive. If smoking is addictive, logic dictates that smokers will be insensitive to price increases.

But the claim also runs counter to what most experts say about how young people smoke. Most young smokers are experimental smokers who do not buy their cigarettes, but instead get them from friends or family, which makes them much less sensitive to high tobacco prices.

Data from the US National Household Survey on Drug Abuse recently showed that over 85 percent of 12–18-year-old smokers consume the three most expensive brands of cigarettes, a fact that is also difficult to square with the claim that young people are price sensitive.

A series of American longitudinal studies has found tax increases have a statistically insignificant effect on preventing young people from smoking. Last year, in a study of tobacco control policies in 27 European countries, it was found that, for adolescents, price was unrelated to smoking prevalence.

Tax increases do succeed, however, in increasing the risk of smoking. Jérôme Adda and Francesca [Cornaglia] of University College London found that a one percent increase in tobacco taxes increases smoking intensity by 0.4 percent, which leads the smoker to inhale more dangerous chemicals and causes cancer deeper in the lung.

The result of public health policy making absent of evidence is tobacco policy that repeatedly fails to address youth smoking. While the government is entitled to its own opinion about the most effective ways to reduce smoking, it is not entitled to its own evidence.

| "Taking all other factors into account— such as whether their parents smoke— seeing a lot of smoking in movies tripled the odds that teens would try smoking."

Smoking in Movies Influences Youth Smoking

Smoke Free Movies

A project of Stanton Glantz, professor of medicine at the University of California, San Francisco, Smoke Free Movies aims to reduce the presence of tobacco products in American motion pictures. It contends in the following viewpoint that smoking in movies influences youths to smoke and to have favorable attitudes toward tobacco. Such depictions account for 44 percent of teens who smoke, the project maintains, and nonsmoking teens whose favorite stars light up on screen are sixteen times more likely to think positively of smoking. With cigarette advertising banned from television, tobacco companies have sought to place their products in motion pictures, the author suggests, as branded and non-branded appearances are a powerful way to recruit new smokers.

As you read, consider the following questions:

1. According to Smoke Free Movies, how much does exposure to smoking in the movies increase the chance that nonsmokers' kids start using tobacco?

2. What industry-wide solution does Smoke Free Movies suggest for limited or no progress at media companies in eliminating smoking from movies?

3. How does Smoke Free Movies respond to tobacco companies' claims that their brands are used in films without their permission?

In 2002, 2004, 2005, 2006, 2008, and 2010 the US Centers for Disease Control and Prevention named tobacco in the movies a major factor in teen smoking. In 2007, the Institute of Medicine of the National Academy of Sciences concluded that:

> Exposure to depictions of smoking in movies is associated with more favorable attitudes toward smoking and characters who smoke, and these positive views are particularly prevalent among youth who themselves smoke.

> Exposure to smoking in movies increases the risk for smoking initiation. Cross-sectional and longitudinal studies provide clear support that youth report greater susceptibility and intentions to smoke and are more likely to actually try smoking following exposure to smoking in the movies and on television. Furthermore, even after controlling for other factors known to be associated with adolescent smoking intention and tobacco use, studies show a clear dose effect, whereby greater exposure to smoking in the movies is associated with a greater chance of smoking.

> The increased risk for smoking initiation as a result of exposure to smoking in the movies can be reduced by anti-smoking advertisements and parental restriction of which movies their children watch.

And, in 2008, after the most comprehensive review of the science to date, the US National Cancer Institute went even further. It concluded:

> The total weight of evidence from cross-sectional, longitudinal, and experimental studies indicates *a causal relationship between exposure to depictions of smoking in movies and youth smoking initiation.*

The research explains why:

- Nonsmoking teens whose favorite stars frequently smoke on screen are sixteen times more likely to have positive attitudes about smoking in the future.

- Smoking in movies is the most powerful pro-tobacco influence on kids today, accounting for 44% of adolescents who start smoking, an effect even stronger than cigarette advertising.

- Taking all other factors into account—such as whether their parents smoke—seeing a lot of smoking in movies tripled the odds that teens would try smoking.

- More important, exposure to smoking in the movies quadrupled the chance that nonsmokers' kids would start.

Big Tobacco's marketing experts and independent researchers agree. Moving stories with charismatic actors are a powerful way to attract new smokers and keep current smokers.

That's why TV advertising of tobacco brands was banned in 1970. Tobacco companies turned to Hollywood to place their brands on screen without the audience knowing. Today, movies that show a tobacco brand are also more likely to include smoking in their TV ads, undercutting the 1970 ban.

Big Tobacco Companies Know the Power of Movies

Marlboros have featured in at least seventy-four of Hollywood's top-grossing movies over the past fifteen years. Studies show that brands showing up on screen most often are also the most heavily advertised in other media.

Insider documents reveal that both Brown and Williamson [Tobacco] and R.J. Reynolds (both now part of British American Tobacco) worried that Philip Morris did a better job of getting its brands, like Marlboro, into the movies. An R.J. Reynolds marketing analyst outlined why smoking in the movies is so important to the tobacco industry:

> "The medium is the message, and the message would be right—part of the show. How different from being the Corporate Moneybags or pushing samples in the lobby. It's the difference between B&W [Brown and Williamson Tobacco] doing commercials in movie houses and Marlboro turning up in the movies."

> "Pull, not push. Nobody tells them the 'answer,' they just know. Not 'why are you smoking that?' but 'I saw that video—can I try one?' If they feel like wearing the badge, they'll buy it. Like magic."

> "Right now, Marlboro has all the magic. And I'm curious how they got it. Certainly legal eyebrows would raise at any direct arrangement for Marlboro's omnipresence in FUBYAS [young smokers] media. In fact, I read recently about a PMer [Philip Morris executive] who was confronted about Marlboro's movie appearances and gave some cagey response like 'Let's just say no money changed hands.' . . . They don't need the magic, but we do—unless we are prepared to wait years for the buzz, much less the payoff on the bottom line."

Studio Survey: Highlights 1999–2008

Analysis of 1,769 films released over the past 18 years established that:

- Most youth exposure to on-screen smoking occurs in youth-rated films, particularly PG-13. In 2008, PG-13 films delivered 65% of tobacco impressions (11.7 billion of the 18.1 billion impressions) and G/PG films delivered another 1% (200 million).

- The fraction of all films that are smoke free has been growing since the late 1990s, yet still remains below 50% even for youth-rated (G/PG/PG-13) films.

- Tobacco incidents per film have fallen by about half since 2005, led by youth-rated films. The total number of tobacco incidents on screen remains above levels seen in the late 1990s.

- The number of films with tobacco brands has, if anything, increased. Marlboro, the brand most frequently chosen by adolescent smokers, was displayed most often—accounting for 75% of brand display in 2008, for example.

By Media Company

- Tobacco incidents have nearly disappeared from Disney's G and PG films.

- In recent years, around 75% of films released by GE (Universal) have featured tobacco—more than from any other major studio. In 2008, tobacco incidents per PG-13 film (on the rise) were as high as incidents per R-rated film (on the decline).

- Tobacco incidents in News Corp. (20th Century Fox) films have been relatively few in recent years. In three out of the last five years, 66% or more of News Corp.'s youth-rated films have been smoke free, a record rivaled only by Disney.

- Sony, one of the largest film producer-distributors, has shown no sustained change in tobacco content since the mid-1990s. No more than 40% of Sony's PG-13 films were smoke free in any year.

- At Warner Bros., the prolific studio owned by Time Warner, tobacco incidents in youth-rated films declined between 2005 and 2007, but the trend reversed in 2008. Over the last three years, the percentage of Time Warner's youth-rated films that were smoke free dropped below 50% to 39%.

- Viacom's Paramount films have ranged between 25% and 50% smoke free since the late 1990s, displaying no real change.

- Independent producer-distributors (large and small) account for a growing number of theatrical releases. In 2008, indies [independent films] included a record number of tobacco incidents in their youth-rated films: twice as many as in 2007 and nearly four times as many as in 2006. By last year, only about one in three youth-rated films released by independents was smoke free.

This film survey's evidence of limited progress at some companies, and none at others, suggests that an industry-wide solution, including R-rating future smoking, is needed to achieve substantial, permanent reductions in dangerous youth exposure to on-screen smoking. . . .

Brand Identification: Wink, Wink, Nudge, Nudge

From 1990 through 2008, at least 180 major U.S. motion pictures displayed or mentioned tobacco brands. In two-thirds of these films, the brands belonged to Philip Morris—mostly Marlboro.

In recent years, total appearances by British American Tobacco brands (Winston, Kool, etc.) have been catching up. But of brands smoked by leading actors on screen, Philip Morris outnumbers British American Tobacco two to one.

Artistic Creativity That Kills

Hollywood does not necessarily have to start a major nonsmoking or drug campaign, although it would not hurt, but simply remove it from the viewing audience. If some writer or producer thinks smoking adds artistic creativity to a scene, they should get a real job that does not cause others to suffer mentally and physically. The harm the writers caused in the black-and-white era in their thrillers and romantic movies, by showing smoking as being sexy, has killed millions of people today.

Alastair Graeme Darrach,
There Is Something Wrong with the World Today.
Bloomington, IN: AuthorHouse, 2007.

Sony, Time Warner, and Viacom Display the Most Brands

Under congressional pressure in 1990, tobacco companies promised not to pay for product placement. 1998's Master Settlement Agreement between domestic tobacco firms and top law enforcement officials made the pledge legally binding. Still, more than 80 percent of tobacco brand appearances in top-grossing movies after 1998 look just like paid placements before 1998: brands from competing companies are kept off screen.

Independent films show few tobacco brands. Ninety percent of U.S. films showing or mentioning tobacco brands have come from major studios owned by media conglomerates, reaching hundreds of millions of viewers around the world.

Of particular interest to law enforcement officials mandated to enforce the Master Settlement Agreement, more than a third of movies (38 percent) identified as displaying tobacco brands have been youth rated.

Branded or Unbranded, Movie Smoking Recruits Teens

Before 1990, tobacco companies publicly claimed that they passively responded to requests for tobacco branding, signage, and other imagery. They lied. Internal documents show they financed a program of product placement agents to get their brands on screen.

Today tobacco giants like Philip Morris claim their brands are used in films without their permission. Unless prodded by law enforcement, however, they do not complain to studios. They have also sent public signals to Hollywood that they won't pursue trademark enforcement action. Meanwhile, Marlboro, the most common brand on screen, continues to be the dominant brand kids smoke.

Brand appearances in movies are valuable to tobacco companies eager to attract new smokers to "starter" brands like Marlboro and Camel. On-screen brands may also play a role in battles for market share in Eastern Europe and Asia. In addition, films showing tobacco brands are significantly more likely to include smoking scenes in their TV ad campaigns, undermining America's four-decade-old ban on tobacco commercials.

Tobacco control experts emphasize that any smoking on screen, branded or unbranded, has a powerful recruitment effect. Since 1999, about 15 percent of movies with smoking have displayed an actual brand: 9 percent of youth-rated films with smoking and 24 percent of R-rated movies with smoking. Philip Morris and BAT [British American Tobacco], the companies with the largest market share, benefit the most when Hollywood shows smoking in the films that adolescents see most—even if their brands show up in a minority of films.

> "The focus on cigarettes with its impli-
> cation that filmmakers should self-
> censor seems a little peculiar given
> what else goes on in films and TV
> shows these days."

Smoking in Movies Should Not Be Censored

Ruby Hamad

Ruby Hamad is a writer and filmmaker based in Sydney, Australia. In the following viewpoint, she insists that smoking in movies is a part of the director's artistic vision and should not be modified or censored. Every fictional aspect—including smoking—intentionally reveals something about the character's personality or state of mind, Hamad says, and eliminating such details can make the movie less believable. She also disagrees with there being a specific focus on cigarettes in movies because other undesirable behaviors and explicit scenes play out on screen. In fact, smoking in movies is not always as endorsement, especially when the character is unlikeable, Hamad contends.

As you read, consider the following questions:

1. How does Hamad respond to the finding that a causal link exists between on-screen smoking and youth smoking?

2. What is the author's opinion of product placement in movies?

3. What is Hamad's view of the filmmaker drawing on the full range of human emotions and behavior?

Only a film director as revered as Woody Allen would have the chutzpah to pull his films from a market as big as India for fear of compromising his artistic vision.

The last time a Hollywood film clashed with paternalistic Indian censors, it was the blockbuster American version of *The Girl with the Dragon Tattoo*, with another famous director, David Fincher, refusing to cut sex scenes (but the violence was okay presumably), which were deemed "unsuitable for public viewing".

There's no sex in *Blue Jasmine* but it is rife with shady business dealings, drinking, and pill popping.

However, it was the two scenes featuring characters smoking cigarettes that caught the eye of Indian authorities.

Indian law dictates that antismoking ads play before every movie, which seems reasonable enough, but, and here's the bit that stuck in Allen's craw, scenes that depict characters smoking must also be modified to include scrolling text warning the audience of the dangers of smoking.

Fearful that the attention of the audience would be diverted (which of course is the entire point), Allen chose instead not to release the film in the subcontinent.

Perhaps it is only fair that authorities tamper with movies given Big Tobacco is known for paying producers big bucks to feature smoking in their films when other avenues for marketing began to close.

Despite the 1998 Master Settlement Agreement, which forbade brand-name tobacco product placement, smoking in movies actually increased until 2005 when it finally began to decline.

Up to 90 per cent of smokers take up the habit before the age of 18 and, in 2012, the US surgeon general found a causal link between on-screen smoking and teenagers taking up the habit. No such relationship exists with adults, however, which begs the question, how many Indian teenagers were likely to watch a wordy comedy-drama about a deluded, middle-aged Park Avenue society queen's fall from grace, anyway?

Not the Concern of the Filmmaker

More to the point, is any of this really the concern of the filmmaker?

I'm certainly not going to suggest that every single film, particularly Hollywood blockbusters, is a work of high art, but as any self-respecting auteur director would tell you, their greatest desire is to 'be true to the story'.

Movies, as we all know, are a meticulously crafted fiction (or at least they aspire to be) but the best of these—such as *Blue Jasmine*—sharply reflect the real world.

When creating characters, every habit, every clothing choice, sleeping position, hairstyle, and household ornament is carefully scrutinised. Nothing, but nothing, is there without a reason.

All of these parts add up to the creation of a believable world. Audiences may not always acknowledge these parts, but they sure as hell miss them when they are not there. And when done exceedingly well, you get a phenomenon of *Breaking Bad* proportions.

What I am getting at is, if a well-developed character smokes in a scene, this is not incidental but is meant to tell us something about the character's personality and state of mind at that moment.

So, as every aghast filmmaker is surely thinking, does the government really have the right to mess with the director's creative vision?

Of course, there is the possibility that Allen would have chosen not to include cigarettes at all had he been aware it would affect his box-office takings, and we'd all be none the wiser to this element of his character's personality.

Nonetheless, the focus on cigarettes with its implication that filmmakers should self-censor seems a little peculiar given what else goes on in films and TV shows these days. Abductions, murders, terrorist plots, chemistry teachers blossoming into drug kingpins. Imagine a message warning of the dangers of cooking meth in your basement infiltrating the bottom of your TV screen every time Walter White donned his yellow hazmat suit and mask.

Not Necessarily an Endorsement

Despite the tendency of some films to go overboard with the product placement (cough, *Man of Steel*, cough), films are not advertisements.

A character doing something in a film is not necessarily an endorsement. In fact, depending on the character, it could be just the opposite.

The most important films tell us something of the human condition, and to do so the filmmaker must draw on the full range of human emotion and behaviour. How unrealistic, not to mention boring, would films be if none of the characters in the fantasy world ever did anything illegal, or immoral, or just plain unhealthy?

Some of the greatest films feature not only the antagonist or peripheral characters but the protagonist doing the most questionable things. In the 2005 Palme d'Or winner *The Child*, Belgian auteurs Jean-Pierr and Luc Dardenne gave us a hero who is a small-time criminal, a loser with mounting debts and a bleak future who sells his own baby to a black market adoption ring.

Clearly, a role model for the ages.

In *Maria Full of Grace*, for which Colombian actress Catalina Sandino Moreno was nominated for an Academy Award, our heroine is a desperate factory worker who resorts to acting as an international drug mule to escape her life of poverty and tedium. She swallows 62 pellets of cocaine and boards a flight to a new life in New York City. Uh, don't try this at home?

Coincidentally, *Maria Full of Grace* was shown in Australia just weeks before news of the Bali Nine [referring to nine Australians arrested for planning to smuggle heroin from Indonesia to Australia] hit the headlines. How's that for life imitating art?

Of course, that's not to excuse gratuitous displays of violence or sex in movies. Or even gratuitous smoking (cough, *Superman Returns*, cough).

But *Blue Jasmine* only has two offending smoking scenes. And by a character so profoundly uncool, he could probably serve as an inspiration to teenagers to quit.

> *"We do not want our brands or brand imagery depicted in movies, television shows or other public entertainment media."*

Tobacco Companies Do Not Promote Smoking in Movies

Philip Morris USA

Philip Morris USA is the nation's largest tobacco manufacturer. In the following viewpoint, the manufacturer declares that it opposes the appearance of its brands and products in movies. Philip Morris USA insists that it refuses all third-party requests to have its imagery—from cigarettes to advertisements—used, shown, or referenced in films and television shows. To increase the entertainment industry's awareness of its policy, the manufacturer claims that it has published advertisements in trade publications, worked with the Motion Picture Association of America to enhance information on smoking in theatrical releases, and reached out to stakeholders at film studios to reiterate its policy and eliminate smoking in movies intended for young audiences.

As you read, consider the following questions:

1. According to Philip Morris USA, what misunderstanding does the unauthorized use of its imagery in movies and television shows perpetuate?

2. In the manufacturer's view, why is it limited in its ability to stop its brands from being displayed in movies?

3. As stated by Philip Morris USA, with whom did it execute engagements to discuss smoking in movies in 2007?

Since 1990, our policy has been to decline all third-party requests to use, display or reference our cigarette brands, products, packages or advertisements in any movies or television shows or other public entertainment media. This policy was reinforced in 1998 by the Master Settlement Agreement (MSA), which strictly prohibits participating manufacturers such as Philip Morris USA [PM USA] from paying for product placement in movies, television shows, other performances or video games.

PM USA's position is clear—we do not want our brands or brand imagery depicted in movies, television shows or other public entertainment media. The unauthorized use of our brands and brand imagery perpetuates the misunderstanding among some that we pay for or are otherwise responsible for these depictions, which is simply not the case.

Research suggests that exposure to cigarette smoking and tobacco in movies may have an impact on youth attitudes and behaviors related to smoking, and consequently, can increase their risk of starting smoking.

Unfortunately, the fact that PM USA does not engage in product placement does not mean that our brands are never shown. Some producers and directors choose to depict PM USA brands in their work without our permission. But we are limited in our ability to stop all displays of our brands, because federal and state trademark laws, as well as the U.S. Constitution, protect freedom of expression and the "fair use" of trademarks in works such as movies and television shows.

Smoking in Movies Is Not Simple

I do not think that it is as simple as stating that smoking in movies in theaters causes 200,000 kids to start smoking each year, or that smoking in movies causes exactly 38% of all smoking initiation. I don't think it is as simple as saying that any depiction of smoking in movies causes kids to smoke. I take a much broader perspective on the problem. I think that the overall widespread exposure in the media to smoking is an influence on smoking initiation. I would be very hesitant to single out one particular mode of exposure and claim that it is single-handedly responsible for all the observed increase in youth smoking among those who are exposed to smoking depictions in that medium.

Michael Siegel,
"In My View: American Legacy Foundation's Call for
R-Rating for Any Movie That Depicts Smoking
Non-Historically Is Hypocritical and Misguided,"
The Rest of the Story: Tobacco News Analysis
and Commentary *(blog), May 11, 2007.*

PM USA believes that producers, directors and others involved in the creative process are in a unique position to voluntarily eliminate smoking scenes in movies and other entertainment media directed at youth, and we encourage them to do so.

Recently, a major National Cancer Institute (2008) review of the literature related to media communications in tobacco promotion and tobacco control concluded that, "The total weight of evidence from cross-sectional, longitudinal, and experimental studies indicates a causal relationship between exposure to movie smoking depictions and youth smoking initiation."

The Stakeholders

In 2004, PM USA began a stakeholder engagement effort to explore our role in helping to achieve a reduction in the amount of smoking scenes in all entertainment programming intended for youth and to help in the elimination of the use of PM USA brand imagery in all entertainment programming.

From 2004 through 2006, PM USA met with more than 20 people and groups who are considered key decision makers in the entertainment industry. Stakeholders included entertainment industry trade organizations, Screen Actors Guild leaders, health advocacy organizations, producers, directors, writers and actors.

What We Heard

There was little awareness among the entertainment industry about our product placement policy, the cigarette industry's MSA restrictions and the impact that depicting smoking in film has on youth smoking. Informing the entertainment industry about the issue could play an important role in gaining their voluntary cooperation to eliminate smoking in movies directed at youth.

How We Responded

In November 2006 and continuing through February 2007, PM USA placed two print advertisements in entertainment industry trade publications. The first was intended to raise awareness of PM USA's position on product placement and the second encouraged the industry to eliminate smoking scenes in movies directed at youth.

In addition, in May of 2007, the Motion Picture Association of America (MPAA) decided to enhance the amount of information provided to parents on the issue of smoking in films. We support the MPAA's decision. Throughout 2007, PM USA executed engagements with major motion picture studios, two minor motion picture studios as well as several key film festivals and trade associations to continue the discussion on eliminating smoking and tobacco use in movies directed at youth.

In 2008, there was another outreach to our key stakeholders at major and minor motion picture studios to reiterate our policies and positions and to encourage them to take additional steps to eliminate smoking scenes in movies directed at youth. In addition, we also held a roundtable discussion with directors, producers and filmmakers at an independent film festival on product placement and the impact of smoking and brand imagery on youth.

PM USA will continue outreach to key stakeholders within the entertainment industry in order to continue to inform them about our efforts. Additionally, we hope to maintain these relationships so that we gain additional insight and feedback to help guide our efforts.

| *"If you take away the look and style of the cigarettes, you will take away the appeal for many young women."*

Plain Packets Will Remove the Appeal of Smoking for Young Women

University of Western Sydney

The following news release issued by the University of Western Sydney, Australia, highlights the research of Dr. Emilee Gilbert. Gilbert, senior lecturer in psychology, finds that plain tobacco packaging reduces the appeal of smoking for young women. Brand imagery and package design, she argues, convey and reinforce positive characteristics about smoking as well as lessen the effectiveness of health warnings in favor of social status and "looking cool." Gilbert asserts the importance of Australians in supporting the change to plain packaging for tobacco products. The University of Western Sydney is a multicampus university in New South Wales, Australia.

As you read, consider the following questions:

1. According to the viewpoint, what did research by Dr. Gilbert reveal about branded cigarette packs?

2. In consumer research, what sort of cigarette packaging did a majority of young women choose, according to the viewpoint?

3. According to Dr. Gilbert's findings, what is initially enticing about smoking?

As the world's first tobacco plain packaging legislation is passed through Parliament today, a researcher from the University of Western Sydney [UWS] says removing the brands from cigarettes is an important step towards deglamorising smoking for young women.

Dr Emilee Gilbert from the School of Psychology at UWS has completed a qualitative study of young women's perceptions and attitudes toward smoking.

The findings clearly indicated that the visual appearance and brands of cigarette packets have a strong influence on people's decisions to take up and continue smoking.

"As smokers often carry their packs with them and keep them on public display, the packaging of the cigarette has become an important vehicle for establishing connections between the brand and the consumer," says Dr Gilbert.

"By taking away the brand of a cigarette packet, you take away this important front line of advertising. We are also stripping the cigarette companies of their ability to lure and establish personal connections between a brand and a consumer."

Dr Gilbert says a prime example of the influence that cigarette brands have on people can be evidenced through the views of young women smokers.

"Since the 1930s, cigarettes have been packaged in slim, long, light-coloured packs to appeal specifically to young women—and the strategy has worked," she says.

"The visual appearance of the cigarette packet is still very important today, with an overwhelming majority of young

"I Would Expect the Model Plain Cigarette Pack to Encourage People to Smoke Less or Quit"

Respondents to the BHF's 2011 polling were asked to consider what packs would encourage people to smoke less or quit. When presented with the Australian-style plain pack with front-facing UK picture warnings, alongside two existing brands, 77 per cent believed that the plain pack would encourage healthier behaviour. A majority of smokers felt the same, with 75 per cent of occasional smokers and 67 per cent of regular smokers feeling the plain packs would encourage people to smoke less or quit.

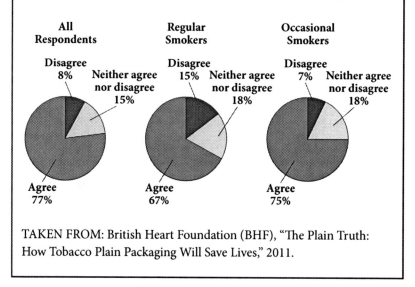

TAKEN FROM: British Heart Foundation (BHF), "The Plain Truth: How Tobacco Plain Packaging Will Save Lives," 2011.

women consistently choosing cigarettes that are sold in light-coloured packages, preferably with a combination of white and gold."

Since the direct advertising of cigarettes has been illegal in Australia, Dr Gilbert says the tobacco industry has become more covert, indirect and subtle in their marketing campaigns—but their efforts have still been successful in attracting young women.

"Despite the proliferation of health messages, many young women in Australia today still consider smoking as a way of looking cool, and attaining a status that is socially valued," says Dr Gilbert.

"It is not the cigarette itself that is initially enticing; it is the image of the cigarette as the ultimate, attainable fashion accessory. If you take away the look and style of the cigarettes, you will take away the appeal for many young women."

Dr Gilbert says it is important for Australians to stand up against tobacco companies and support the change.

"It is no wonder the tobacco industry is so strongly opposed to the plain packaging legislation, because they are incredibly aware of the influence that brands have on people," she says.

> "Enforcing plain packaging on tobacco products would have detrimental consequences on legal producers and their brands, without reducing the consumption of tobacco."

Plain Tobacco Packaging Would Have Unintended Consequences

Michel Kelly-Gagnon and Youri Chassin

In the following viewpoint, Michel Kelly-Gagnon and Youri Chassin argue that plain tobacco packaging would have various unintended consequences. Kelly-Gagnon and Chassin state that studies favoring plain packaging do not consider other factors that impact youth smoking and include erroneous correlations between brand recognition and cigarette brand consumption. More importantly, generic packs would actually increase smoking by diminishing the premium of brands, which would lower cigarette prices and attract additional smokers, they explain. The authors conclude that plain packaging would be detrimental to legitimate businesses without achieving its goal. Kelly-Gagnon is president and chief executive officer of the Montreal Economic Institute (MEI) in Montreal, Canada. Chassin is an economist at MEI.

As you read, consider the following questions:

1. What are the benefits of branding, as claimed by the authors?

2. Why do proponents of plain packaging realize that its effects would be marginal, according to Kelly-Gagnon and Chassin?

3. What evidence do the authors cite to support their argument that plain packaging would increase smoking?

Plain packaging means removing all distinctive elements (logo, colours, lettering) associated with a product and replacing them with a generic package usually including government-mandated warnings (related to health or the environment). For example, a cigarette package would indicate only the brand in small letters that would be standardized for all companies.

Some governments, including those in New Zealand and the U.K. [United Kingdom], are considering the possibility of introducing legislation to mandate plain packaging in the case of cigarettes. The Australian government plans to implement such a requirement by July 2012. The federal government of Canada, which considered and rejected plain packaging 15 years ago, announced last December [in 2010] that it was increasing the size of the compulsory health warning from 50% to 75% of the space on cigarette packages, a measure that reduces, in a roundabout way, the distinctiveness of cigarette brands.

While empirical research is inconclusive as to the actual effectiveness of this approach, some studies suggest that plain packaging could on the contrary have unintended negative consequences. It is a classic case of a policy that focuses on "that which is seen" and ignores "that which is not seen" directly.

The Importance of Brand Names

Plain packaging, by prohibiting the visual elements that allow consumers to differentiate products, would hamper brand recognition. The benefits of branding, though, are well understood. From the consumer's point of view, the function of a brand name is to convey information about a producer's reputation. Consumers rely on brand names because they know that the producers to whom they belong have an incentive to maintain the quality of their products in order to preserve the value of their brands. In other words, brands simplify choices.

For these reasons, consumers are usually willing to pay more for brand-name products than for generic products. They pay more for used cars with brands associated with higher quality. Similarly, they pay a premium for brand-name prescription drugs as opposed to generic drugs, for brand-name clothes, etc. When retailers—grocery stores, for example—eschew well-known brands, they often replace them with their own "private labels."

Because of this consumer attachment, brand names are worth a lot to producers. In 2008, for example, the "Guinness World Records" brand was sold for £60 million (nearly CAN$118 million). . . .

Will Plain Packaging Reduce Tobacco Consumption?

Efforts to promote plain packaging emphasize the goal of reducing tobacco consumption and youth smoking initiation rates. Since no country has yet imposed plain packaging for cigarettes, the scientific literature on this subject offers no definitive conclusions. Analyses of the impact of such a measure usually rely on interviews, focus groups and experiments on recognizing and recalling cigarette brand names. A number of such studies have been carried out over the years. But a review of 13 major public health studies that had found a potentially effective impact of plain packaging on smoking (and especially on youth smoking) has exposed major flaws in those studies. Their results are ambiguous at best, and moreover do not support their conclusions.

First, the studies often limit themselves to showing that consumers have a positive evaluation of brands, or that health warnings are more readily noticed on a generic package, without actually showing that such factors have a determining influence on tobacco consumption.

Also, the studies in favour of generic packaging do not follow the recognized methods of statistical analysis, which are required to demonstrate a causal link in the social sciences. They do not consider other factors that have an impact on youth smoking decisions—cigarette prices, parent and peer influence, access, etc.—and that are potentially more important than packaging. Such factors could reduce or completely cancel out the alleged positive impact of plain packaging.

Finally, many of the studies reviewed show spurious correlations. A classic example of this unfortunate methodological error is provided by the positive correlation between drownings at sea and ice cream sales. Even though the correlation is real, it would be absurd to deduce that ice cream causes drowning. Rather, the positive correlation arises because both variables are correlated with a third, hidden variable: warm summer weather. Similarly, an apparent correlation between cigarette brand recognition and the consumption of branded cigarettes could very well depend on the action of a third causal variable like peer influence.

To sum up, the direct consequence of these methodological shortcomings is that no causal relation has been established between plain packaging of cigarettes and tobacco consumption. In other words, there is no scientific basis for the promotion of plain packaging.

Proponents of plain packaging have long realized that its effects would be at best marginal, as illustrated by an expert panel study commissioned by Health Canada, whose conclusions are ambivalent. Indeed, a large part of the "evidence" reported was based on the opinions of teenagers interviewed in a mall. Half of them thought that plain packaging would not reduce the number of teenagers who decide to start smoking cigarettes, and just 5.6% thought it was the best way to stop youths from smoking. The study concludes that, "generic packaging will not have major effects," but nonetheless states that "it will be another nail in the coffin of smoking."

The Real Impact of Packaging on Tobacco Consumption

More useful are indirect studies that use actual health warnings as a proxy for plain packaging. Indeed, if plain packaging is to have an impact, existing health warnings, which amount to partial plain packaging, should have had some impact, too. On the contrary, however, studies show that these health warnings have had no impact.

An econometric study of the Canadian case highlights the fact that one year after appearing on Canadian packs of cigarettes in 2001, aggressive, graphic health warnings had had no statistically significant effect on the proportion of smokers in the population, even in the 15–19 age group.

Health warnings on tobacco products have long been much more visible in Canada than in the United States. These warnings have occupied 20% of the front of each package since 1989, and 50% since 2001, compared to around 5% in the United States, usually on the side of the package.

Logically, smoking rates should be lower in Canada since these warnings became more visible, if we adjust for other factors related to demographics, price and other variables.

Is Packaging a Reason Why People Start Smoking?

All the evidence suggests not. Only 1% of UK [United Kingdom] smokers cite packaging as one of the various factors in their decision to start smoking. Research regularly shows the most important factors involved in smoking initiation include

• rebelliousness;

• risk taking;

• family structure, parental example;

• relationships, peer pressure;

• socioeconomic status;

• school connection; and,

• educational success.

Imperial Tobacco, "The Evidence Is Plain: The Ineffectiveness of Standardised Packaging for Public Health," January 10, 2014.

This is not, however, what is observed. Smoking rates in the United States, for young and old alike, have not been higher than in Canada in the last two decades, despite the less visible health warnings. These health warnings have therefore clearly not produced the kinds of results expected.

The Real Consequences

Cigarette packages have recently been attacked by prohibiting the display of tobacco at points of sales in Canada, Thailand, Iceland and Ireland. In the Canadian provinces, these prohibitions have led to the closure of hundreds of small convenience stores. However, they have had no discernable impact on smoking rates. They have merely encouraged smokers to buy their cigarettes at the supermarket (convenience stores no longer being able to display their range of available products) and especially to buy contraband cigarettes. With the prohibition of advertising, including at points of sales, packaging remains the main method of branding, if not the only one, still available to cigarette producers.

As with the display ban, there is a strong chance that plain packaging for cigarettes would entail unintended negative consequences without achieving its declared objective of improving the health of the population. Indeed, if consumers cannot rely on a brand as a warranty of quality and reputation, they will not be willing to pay a premium for those products. Concretely, plain packaging would reduce the brand premium and therefore the price of brand cigarettes. The consumption of tobacco would not fall, but cigarette manufacturers that have invested in establishing their reputations would be harmed. The distinction between the goal of reducing smoking and that of needlessly harming legitimate corporations is important here because the latter is clearly no longer a public health issue. Plain packaging would harm manufacturers just as the display ban harmed convenience stores, all without improving anybody's health.

In fact, by abolishing the brand premium, we can predict that sales will increase, according to the law of demand.

According to a simulation on brand value carried out in Australia, prices would fall by 5% to 19%. Using conservative estimates for the Canadian market, we can predict that the reduction of the price of cigarettes resulting from a plain packaging policy would lead to the addition of 135,000 extra smokers (there are currently 4.8 million), an increase of nearly 3%. Although estimates are approximate by nature, logic dictates that a decrease in the price of cigarettes caused by the disappearance of brand names could provoke an increase in tobacco consumption.

Thus, unless plain packaging succeeded in compensating for this probable increase, which it likely would not according to the current scientific literature, the adoption of this measure would have the opposite effect of what is intended.

More Negative than Positive Consequences

The existing scientific literature does not establish a causal link between plain packaging and tobacco consumption. In the absence of proof, any implementation would at best represent merely a shot in the dark as far as public health is concerned, and unfortunately risks provoking consequences that are more negative than positive.

What the available evidence does show is that enforcing plain packaging on tobacco products would have detrimental consequences on legal producers and their brands, without reducing the consumption of tobacco. On the contrary, instead of reducing health risks, this policy would achieve the exact opposite of its stated purpose by leading to an increase in the number of smokers. It would not be the first time that a seemingly well-intentioned policy produces harmful unintended consequences.

Moreover, tobacco may be just the first victim in a global attack on branding. Other products deemed "sinful" may well be targeted in the future: fast food, alcohol, lottery tickets (although the two latter cases currently enjoy the sanction of the Quebec government), etc.

In economics, the availability of information is important. However, once the risks of using a product are known, to what extent does the government need to interfere with the choices of individuals in order to protect them from themselves? If everybody already knows that cigarettes cause health problems—and even impotence!—could we respect the choices of those who adopt this behaviour, even if this decision remains inscrutable to some?

Periodical and Internet Sources Bibliography

The following articles have been selected to supplement the diverse views presented in this chapter.

Sarah Boseley	"England to Introduce Plain Packaging for Cigarettes," *Guardian*, April 3, 2014.
Erin Brodwin	"Tobacco Companies Still Target Youth Despite a Global Treaty," *Scientific American*, October 21, 2013.
Michelle Castillo	"Plain Cigarette Packaging May Encourage More Smokers to Quit," CBS News, July 23, 2013.
Stephen Cheliotis	"Opinion: Australian Tobacco Packaging Laws Misguided," CNN, August 15, 2012.
Murali Doraiswamy	"Stop Glamorizing Drugs and Smoking in Movies and Songs," *Wall Street Journal*, September 17, 2014.
Economist	"Look What They've Done to My Brands," November 17, 2012.
Amanda Gardner	"Should Smoking Trigger an R Rating?," CNN, July 13, 2012.
Gerard Gilbert	"Smoking in Films: Light Up, Camera, Action," *Independent* (London), January 14, 2014.
Genevra Pittmann	"Smoking in Movies May Turn Teens to Cigarettes: Study," *Chicago Tribune*, July 9, 2012.
RAND Corporation	"Influence of Pro-Smoking Media Messages Lasts 7 Days, Study Finds," ScienceDaily, November 18, 2013.
Eric Schwartzel	"Coming Soon to Theaters Near You: E-Cigarettes," *Wall Street Journal*, September 14, 2014.

For Further Discussion

Chapter 1

1. The US Department of Health and Human Services states that one million Americans become new smokers every year. However, the Federal Trade Commission claims that the number of cigarettes sold or given away has dropped more than forty billion between 2008 and 2010. In your view, which claim is more persuasive in describing the prevalence of smoking in the United States? Explain your answer.

2. The American Cancer Society maintains that 23 percent of high school students have used other forms of tobacco products within the past month. On the other hand, L.D. Johnston and his colleagues suggest that such tobacco use among teens is modestly declining or leveling off after increasing. In your opinion, which viewpoint provides the more convincing evidence on the issue? Explain, citing examples from the viewpoints to support your response.

3. Frances Robert Lato relies on anecdotal evidence regarding the dangers of secondhand smoke. In your view, is using anecdotal evidence an effective way to present an argument against tobacco? Why, or why not?

Chapter 2

1. The Campaign for Tobacco-Free Kids asserts that rising cigarette prices are correlated with lower smoking rates. Nonetheless, Diana Oprinescu says that consumers supplant cigarettes with alternatives that are taxed less. In your opinion, who presents the stronger argument? Use examples from the viewpoints to support your answer.

2. Ronald Bayer in his interview with Sarah Clune insists that smoking bans are intended to protect smokers from

themselves rather than the public from secondhand smoke. Do you agree with Bayer's argument? Why, or why not?

3. John Kruzel writes about Needham, Massachusetts, as a success story in raising the smoking age to twenty-one to reduce smoking. In your opinion, does Eric Levenson in his viewpoint successfully counter Kruzel's argument? Cite examples from the viewpoints to support your response.

Chapter 3

1. Gilbert Ross maintains that nicotine replacement therapies provide an unacceptably low level of assistance in smoking cessation. Does Ross's argument convince you that electronic cigarettes should not be federally regulated? Use examples from the viewpoint to support your answer.

2. Christopher Wanjek believes that converting smokers into "vapers" is not a step toward better health. Do you agree with the author? Why, or why not?

3. The Centers for Disease Control and Prevention (CDC) suggests applying smoking bans to smokeless tobacco products. In your opinion, without secondhand smoke, is banning smokeless tobacco in public or workplaces fair? Why, or why not?

Chapter 4

1. The Center for Public Health and Tobacco Policy argues that research demonstrates that tobacco marketing influences youth smoking. On the contrary, Patrick Basham maintains that research fails to establish a significant link between advertising and smoking rates among young people. In your view, which author offers stronger evidence? Cite examples from the viewpoints to support your response.

2. Ruby Hamad claims that as a part of the filmmaker's creative vision, smoking in movies should not be censored or modified. Do you agree with the author? Why, or why not?

3. Michel Kelly-Gagnon and Youri Chassin argue that plain packaging on cigarettes would actually increase smoking by diminishing the premium of brands, which would lower cigarette prices and attract additional smokers. On the other hand, Emilee Gilbert of the University of Western Sydney thinks that plain tobacco packaging would reduce the appeal of smoking, especially for young women. With which viewpoint do you agree, and why?

Organizations to Contact

The editors have compiled the following list of organizations concerned with the issues debated in this book. The descriptions are derived from materials provided by the organizations. All have publications or information available for interested readers. The list was compiled on the date of publication of the present volume; the information provided here may change. Be aware that many organizations take several weeks or longer to respond to inquiries, so allow as much time as possible.

Action on Smoking and Health (ASH)
701 Fourth Street NW, Washington, DC 20001
(202) 659-4310
website: www.ash.org

Action on Smoking and Health (ASH) is a nonprofit organization fighting for the rights of nonsmokers through legal action and educational initiatives. ASH has worked to eliminate tobacco ads from many media outlets and to ban smoking on public transportation and in many public places. It publishes the e-newsletter *Action Review*, and the *ASH Blog* features entries such as "Should E-Cigarettes Be Considered Tobacco Products?"

American Cancer Society (ACS)
250 Williams Street NW, Atlanta, GA 30303
(800) 227-2345
website: www.cancer.org

Founded in 1913, the American Cancer Society (ACS) is a nationwide voluntary organization focused on cancer as a public health issue. ACS educates the public about the dangers of smoking and lobbies for antismoking legislation. ACS makes available on its website numerous publications, ranging from position papers and surveys to reports, including "The Landmark Surgeon General Report on Smoking and Health, 50 Years Later," "Ewwww, That's Gross! A New Era in U.S. Cigarette Labeling," and "Hookahs Are Trendy, but Are They Safe?"

American Council on Science and Health (ACSH)

1995 Broadway, Suite 202, New York, NY   10023-5882
(866) 905-2694 • fax: (212) 362-4919
e-mail: acsh@acsh.org
website: www.acsh.org

The American Council on Science and Health (ACSH) is a consumer education group concerned with public policies related to health and the environment. ACSH works to add reason and balance to debates about public health issues, such as tobacco use. Its website provides many publications, position statements, and articles, including "Health Effects of Menthol in Cigarettes," "'E-Cigarettes Encourage Teen Smoking!' No, They Don't in Fact," and "The Effects of Nicotine on Human Health."

American Lung Association

55 W. Wacker Drive, Suite 1150, Chicago, IL   60601
(800) 586-4872 • fax: (202) 452-1805
website: www.lung.org

Founded in 1904, the American Lung Association is the leading organization working to improve lung health and prevent lung disease. Through education, advocacy, and research, the association fights for healthy lungs and healthy air. The organization publishes the annual "State of Tobacco Control," along with other reports such as "Big Tobacco's Guinea Pigs." It supports the Quitter in You smoking cessation campaign, which aims to help individuals break the habit of nicotine addiction.

Americans for Nonsmokers' Rights (ANR)

2530 San Pablo Avenue, Suite J, Berkeley, CA   94702
(510) 841-3032 • fax: (510) 841-3071
website: www.no-smoke.org

Americans for Nonsmokers' Rights (ANR) is a national lobbying organization. Through an action-oriented program of policy and legislation, it takes on the tobacco industry at all levels of government, protects nonsmokers from exposure to secondhand smoke, and prevents tobacco addiction among youth. It publishes the quarterly newsletter *ANR UPDATE* and provides links to online articles that discuss topics such as the dangers of secondhand smoke, the economic impact of smoke-free laws, and scientific research on smoking and air quality.

Campaign for Tobacco-Free Kids

1400 I Street NW, Suite 1200, Washington, DC   20005
(202) 296-5469
e-mail: info@tobaccofreekids.org
website: www.tobaccofreekids.org

The Campaign for Tobacco-Free Kids is a nonprofit organization that advocates for public policies that prevent youth smoking, promote smoking cessation, and reduce secondhand smoke. Available at its website are fact sheets and reports, including "Toll of Tobacco in the U.S.A." and "Raising Cigarette Taxes Reduces Smoking, Especially Among Kids (And the Cigarette Companies Know It)." Its website also features a blog, *Tobacco Unfiltered*, which provides news and information about the worldwide movement to reduce tobacco use.

Cato Institute

1000 Massachusetts Avenue NW
Washington, DC   20001-5403
(202) 842-0200
website: www.cato.org

The Cato Institute is a public policy research foundation dedicated to limiting the role of government, protecting individual liberties, and promoting free markets. Its scholars conduct independent research and provide analysis on vital public policy issues. Among its publications are the quarterly magazine *Regulation*, the bimonthly *Cato Policy Report*, and the triannual *Cato Journal*. Articles such as "Smoking Stupidity," "Terror Campaign Directed at Smoking Applies a Faulty Logic," and "Do Anti-Smoking Programs Work to Reduce Smoking?" can be found on the organization's website.

Competitive Enterprise Institute (CEI)

1899 L Street NW, 12th Floor, Washington, DC   20036
(202) 331-1010 • fax: (202) 331-0640
e-mail: info@cei.org
website: www.cei.org

Founded in 1984, the Competitive Enterprise Institute (CEI) is a nonprofit public policy organization dedicated to free enterprise, limited government, and individual liberty. CEI's publications include policy studies, newsletters, and articles such as "Regulating E-Cigarettes Creates the Wrong Incentives" and "Congress, Tobacco, and a President Who Lights Up."

FORCES International

PO Box 4267, Kaneohe, HI   96744
(808) 721-8384
e-mail: info@forces.org
website: www.forces.org

FORCES International is a nonprofit educational organization that supports human rights and the defense of the freedom to smoke, eat, drink and enjoy personal lifestyle choices without restrictions and state interference. FORCES promotes the value of individual liberty in personal choices and fights against smoking ordinances and restrictions designed to eventually eliminate smoking. Its website includes articles about smoking and tobacco products, including "Alternative Tobacco Products" and "Fighting Smoking Bans."

Foundation for Economic Education (FEE)

1718 Peachtree Street NW, Suite 1048, Atlanta, GA   30309
(800) 960-4333
e-mail: support@fee.org
website: www.fee.org

The Foundation for Economic Education (FEE) is a free market organization that promotes private property rights, the free market economic system, and limited government. The organization publishes a monthly journal, the *Freeman*, which features many articles opposing regulation of the tobacco industry and opposing smoking bans, including "Tobacco Speakeasy."

Legacy

1724 Massachusetts Avenue NW, Washington, DC   20036

(202) 454-5555

website: www.legacyforhealth.org

Legacy is a nonprofit organization dedicated to building a world where young people reject tobacco products. The organization supports the Truth campaign, a national tobacco youth prevention and education program. Legacy conducts extensive research on tobacco-related issues and publishes the results in its "First Look Reports," a series of brief summaries of its research. Legacy also publishes a monthly e-newsletter, *The Ripple Effect*, as well as disseminates press releases, such as "44 Percent of Adolescents Who Start Smoking Do So Because of Smoking Images They Have Seen in the Movies."

National Institute on Drug Abuse (NIDA)

6001 Executive Boulevard, Room 5213

Bethesda, MD   20892-9561

(301) 443-1124

website: www.drugabuse.gov

The National Institute on Drug Abuse (NIDA), one of the National Institutes of Health (NIH), is part of the United States Department of Health and Human Services. NIDA supports and conducts research on drug abuse, including the yearly Monitoring the Future survey, to improve addiction prevention, treatment, and policy efforts. It publishes the bimonthly *NIDA Notes* newsletter, along with public education materials, including the research report "Tobacco" and the drug fact sheet "Electronic Cigarettes (e-Cigarettes)."

Reason Foundation

5737 Mesmer Avenue, Los Angeles, CA   90230
(310) 391-2245 • fax: (310) 391-4395
website: www.reason.org

The Reason Foundation is a nonprofit organization advocating free markets and individual liberty. Founded in 1978, it promotes choice, competition, and a dynamic market economy as the foundation for human dignity and progress. It publishes the monthly *Reason* magazine, and its website features articles such as "Proposed L.A. E-Cigarette Ban Would Perpetuate Smoking, Not Discourage It."

US Environmental Protection Agency (EPA)

1200 Pennsylvania Avenue NW, Washington, DC   20460
(202) 272-0167
website: www.epa.gov

The Environmental Protection Agency (EPA) is the agency of the US government that was created to protect human health and safeguard the natural environment. The EPA's Smoke-Free Homes program promotes indoor air free from environmental tobacco smoke. The EPA publishes numerous fact sheets and brochures, including "Secondhand Tobacco Smoke and the Health of Your Family."

Bibliography of Books

Bennett Abney and Aaron E. Christopherson, eds. *Cigarette and Tobacco Taxes: Effects on Health, Revenues, and the Federal Budget.* New York: Nova Science, 2012.

Patrick Basham and John Luik *The Plain Truth: Does Packaging Influence Smoking?* Washington, DC: Democracy Institute, 2012.

Peter Bearman, Kathryn M. Neckerman, and Leslie Wright, eds. *After Tobacco; What Would Happen if Americans Stopped Smoking?* New York: Columbia University Press, 2011.

Virginia Berridge *Demons: Our Changing Attitudes to Alcohol, Tobacco, and Drugs.* New York: Oxford University Press, 2013.

Allan M. Brandt *The Cigarette Century: The Rise, Fall, and Deadly Persistence of the Product That Defined America.* New York: Basic Books, 2009.

Paul Cairney, Donley T. Studlar, and Hadii M. Mamudu *Global Tobacco Control: Power, Policy, Governance and Transfer.* New York: Palgrave Macmillan, 2012.

John Castle *Smokeless: An Introductory Guide to the Pleasures of Vaping.* Seattle, WA: CreateSpace, 2013.

Zachary Chastain *Tobacco: Through the Smoke Screen.* Broomall, PA: Mason Crest, 2013.

Eric Coates	*Smoking: An Intimate History.* Seattle, WA: CreateSpace, 2014.
Michael Eriksen, Judith Mackay, and Hana Ross	*The Tobacco Atlas.* 4th ed. Atlanta, GA: American Cancer Society, 2012.
Stuart L. Esrock, Kandi L. Walker, and Joy L. Hart, eds.	*Talking Tobacco: Interpersonal, Organizational, and Mediated Messages.* New York: Peter Lang Publishing Inc., 2014.
Michael S. Givel and Andrew L. Spivak	*Heartland Tobacco War.* Lanham, MD: Lexington Books, 2013.
Chris Harrald and Fletcher Watkins	*The Cigarette Book: The History and Culture of Smoking.* New York: Skyhorse Publishing, 2010.
Justin Healey	*Tobacco Smoking.* Thirroul, Australia: Spinney Press, 2011.
Geraint Howells	*The Tobacco Challenge: Legal Policy and Consumer Protection.* Burlington, VT: Ashgate, 2011.
Theodore J. King	*The War on Smokers and the Rise of the Nanny State.* Bloomington, IN: iUniverse, 2009.
Joyce Libal	*Putting Out the Fire: Smoking and the Law.* Broomall, PA: Mason Crest, 2008.
Ann Malaspina	*False Images, Deadly Promises: Smoking and the Media.* Broomall, PA: Mason Crest, 2008.

Ronald Markowitz and Jennifer Galucci, eds.   *Cigarettes and Smokeless Tobacco: Sales and Advertising Statistics and Trends.* New York: Nova Science, 2013.

Pamela E. Pennock   *Advertising Sin and Sickness: The Politics of Alcohol and Tobacco Marketing, 1950–1990.* DeKalb: Northern Illinois University Press, 2009.

Robert N. Proctor   *Golden Holocaust: Origins of the Cigarette Catastrophe and the Case for Abolition.* Los Angeles: University of California Press, 2011.

Brad Rodu   *For Smokers Only: How Smokeless Tobacco Can Save Your Life.* Hermosa Beach, CA: Sumner Books, 2014.

Katie John Sharp   *Smokeless Tobacco: Not a Safe Alternative.* Broomall, PA: Mason Crest, 2009.

Christopher Snowdon   *Velvet Glove, Iron Fist: A History of Anti-Smoking.* North Yorkshire, England: Little Dice, 2009.

Tania Voon, Andrew D. Mitchell, and Jonathan Liberman, eds.   *Public Health and Plain Packaging of Cigarettes.* Northampton, MA: Edward Elgar, 2012.

Richard White   *Smoke Screens: The Truth About Tobacco.* Raleigh, NC: Lulu, 2009.

Index

social, environmental, cognitive, genetic influences, 25
tobacco facts, 35–38
tobacco use, health consequences, 23–24
usage rates, price correlation, 79

See also High school students; Middle school students

Z

Zeller, Mitch, 150
Zyban (bupropion), 142